AMERICAN WAR LIBRARY

★ ★ ★ ★

★ **The Vietnam War** ★

WEAPONS OF WAR

Titles in The American War Library series include:

World War II
Hitler and the Nazis
Kamikazes
Leaders and Generals
Life as a POW
Life of an American Soldier in
  Europe
Strategic Battles in Europe
Strategic Battles in the Pacific
The War at Home
Weapons of War

The Civil War
Leaders of the North and South
Life Among the Soldiers and
  Cavalry
Lincoln and the Abolition of
  Slavery

Strategic Battles
Weapons of War

The Persian Gulf War
Leaders and Generals
Life of an American Soldier
The War Against Iraq
Weapons of War

The Vietnam War
A History of U.S. Involvement
The Home Front: Americans
  Protest the War
Leaders and Generals
Life as a POW
Life of an American Soldier
Weapons of War

AMERICAN
WAR LIBRARY

★ ★ ★ ★

★ The Vietnam War ★

WEAPONS
OF WAR

Lucent Books, P.O. Box 289011, San Diego, CA 92198-9011

To Staff Sergeant Robert P. Daniels, USAF,
52nd Tactical Fighter Wing, a "Phantom Phixer."

Library of Congress Cataloging-in-Publication Data

Weapons of war
      p. cm.—(American war library: Vietnam War)
Includes bibliographical references and index.
  ISBN 1-56006-719-5 (hard : alk. paper)
1. Vietnamese Conflict, 1961–1975—Equipment and supplies
    —Juvenile literature. 2. Vietnamese Conflict, 1961–1975—Technology
—Juvenile literature. 3. Military weapons—Vietnam—History—20th
century—Juvenile literature. [1. Vietnamese Conflict, 1961–1975. 2. Military weapons.] I. Title. II. Series.
  DS559.8.S9 R53 2001
  959.704'34'028—dc21

                                                              00-009557

Copyright 2001 by Lucent Books, Inc.
P.O. Box 289011, San Diego, California 92198-9011

Printed in the U.S.A.

★ Contents ★

A Nation Forged by War

The United States, like many nations, was forged and defined by war. Despite Benjamin Franklin's opinion that "There never was a good war or a bad peace," the United States owes its very existence to the War of Independence, one to which Franklin wholeheartedly subscribed. The country forged by war in 1776 was tempered and made stronger by the Civil War in the 1860s.

The Texas Revolution, the Mexican-American War, and the Spanish-American War expanded the country's borders and gave it overseas possessions. These wars made the United States a world power, but this status came with a price, as the nation became a key but reluctant player in both World War I and World War II.

Each successive war further defined the country's role on the world stage. Following World War II, U.S. foreign policy redefined itself to focus on the role of defender, not only of the freedom of its own citizens, but also of the freedom of people everywhere. During the cold war that followed World War II until the collapse of the Soviet Union, defending the world meant fighting communism. This goal, manifested in the Korean and Vietnam conflicts, proved elusive, and soured the American public on its achievability. As the United States emerged as the world's sole superpower, American foreign policy has been guided less by national interest and more on protecting international human rights. But as involvement in Somalia and Kosovo prove, this goal has been equally elusive.

As a result, the country's view of itself changed. Bolstered by victories in World Wars I and II, Americans first relished the role of protector. But, as war followed war in a seemingly endless procession, Americans began to doubt their leaders, their motives, and themselves. The Vietnam War especially caused people to question the validity of sending its young people to die in places where they were not particularly wanted and for people who did not seem especially grateful.

While the most obvious changes brought about by America's wars have been geopolitical in nature, many other aspects of society have been touched. War often does not bring about change directly, but acts instead like the catalyst in a chemical reaction, accelerating changes already in progress.

Some of these changes have been societal. The role of women in the United States had been slowly changing, but World War II put thousands into the workforce and into uniform. They might have gone back to being housewives after the war, but equality, once experienced, would not be forgotten.

Likewise, wars have accelerated technological change. The necessity for faster airplanes and a more destructive bomb led to the development of jet planes and nuclear energy. Artificial fibers developed for parachutes in the 1940s were used in the clothing of the 1950s.

Lucent Books' American War Library covers key wars in the development of the nation. Each war is covered in several volumes, to allow for more detail, context, and to provide volumes on often neglected subjects, such as the kamikazes of World War II, or weapons used in the Civil War. As with all Lucent Books, notes, annotated bibliographies, and appendixes such as glossaries give students a launching point for further research. In addition, sidebars and archival photographs enhance the text. Together, each volume in The American War Library will aid students in understanding how America's wars have shaped and changed its politics, economics, and society.

The Vietnam Experience

American involvement in Vietnam can be traced back to 1950, when President Harry S. Truman's administration began to lend heavy support to France's campaign to preserve its colonial empire in what was then known as French Indochina. By 1953, the United States had assumed 80 percent of France's cost in the First Indochina War (1946–1954). Following the French defeat at Dien Bien Phu on May 7, 1954, by communist leader Ho Chi Minh's Vietminh (League for Vietnamese Independence) insurgents, the Geneva Conference of 1954 divided Vietnam into North and South Vietnam. War erupted five years later in South Vietnam, when the communist-led Viet Cong guerrillas (commonly referred to as the VC or "Charlie") attempted to overthrow the U.S.-supported South Vietnamese government and reunite the two Vietnams under a communist regime.

In October 1961, President John F. Kennedy, concerned about communist gains in South Vietnam, sent his personal military advisor Gen. Maxwell D. Taylor to Vietnam to assess the situation. Within a week Taylor wired an urgent "eyes only" cable to the president recommending an immediate deployment of U.S. troops to establish a "military presence capable of showing to Southeast Asia the seriousness of the US intent to resist a Communist takeover."[1]

National security advisor McGeorge Bundy concurred with Taylor, stating that sending combat troops had "become a touchstone of American will." He recommended a limited U.S. commitment of one division, after which, he speculated, "the odds are almost even that the commitment will not have to be carried out."[2]

But not all Kennedy administration officials favored a troop commitment in Southeast Asia. Abraham Chayes, state department legal advisor, cautioned that if the president authorized the use of U.S. combat troops in Vietnam he must stand ready

Beginning with only a handful of advisors, the U.S. presence in Vietnam eventually reached over 500,000 combat troops.

to "escalate, if necessary, to the dimensions of a Korea-type conflict."[3]

History has shown the validity of Chayes's warning. America's troop commitment began with a trickle of military advisors under President Kennedy in 1961. By the time of his death in 1963, the number of U.S. advisors in Vietnam had ballooned to 16,700. Under President Lyndon B. Johnson U.S. troop strength in Vietnam steadily rose to a peak of 550,000 in 1969.

A Vast Display of Weaponry

The Vietnam War (called the Second Indochina War by some historians and the American War by the Vietnamese) dragged on with direct U.S. participation until 1973 and indirect advisory and administrative participation thereafter until the final collapse of the Saigon (South Vietnamese) government in 1975. The conflict claimed more than fifty-eight thousand American lives and holds the dubious distinction of being the longest (and arguably the strangest) war ever fought by Americans.

Three decades of conflict in Vietnam (including the First Indochina War) gave witness to every form of modern warfare, excepting nuclear weapons, ranging from shadowy guerrilla warfare to full-blown conventional war. Weaponry employed by the belligerents ran an unlikely gamut from crude homemade bombs to bombers designed to deliver nuclear payloads. The United States armed and equipped itself and its South Vietnamese allies with virtually every weapon, save nuclear, in the prodigious American arsenal. On the other side, the Soviet Union and several of its satellite nations and the People's Republic of China supplied the People's Army of Vietnam (PAVN)—better known as the North Vietnamese Army (NVA)—and the Viet Cong with a broad array of weaponry.

Too Much Technology?

Many military authorities and warfare analysts contend that the French and American campaigns in Vietnam following World War II suffered from an overdose of technology. Both the French and the Americans, they claim, relied on advanced technology to compensate for their deficiencies in manpower and tactical ability. Some experts further contend that the United States employed vast numbers of high-tech weapons simply because they existed. For example, they say, the American arsenal included so many helicopters that it became virtually impossible for American strategists *not* to use them.

Although U.S. technology enabled American troops to attack or defend with a speed, force, and precision their enemy could not match, the high-tech superiority of U.S. forces and their allies often backfired in Vietnam. As a case in point, the Viet Cong would often incite an incident in a village to provoke an American response, then quickly disappear into the countryside. The Americans would answer the VC provocation with shelling or bombing, killing and injuring only innocent civilians. The result of such tactically well-intentioned but misdirected displays of American force served only to aggravate local populations. Because the war in Vietnam was a political conflict fought over the control of the Vietnamese people, such incidents seriously impaired relations with those whom the Americans were trying to help.

The Crucible of War

Apart from the political aspects of the long struggle in Vietnam, the war served as a massive proving ground for the Americans and the Soviets to test their latest weaponry and tactics. For the most part, their developing arsenals had evolved through several previous conflicts, primarily in Korea and the Middle East. But Vietnam demonstrated that the lessons and tactics of past wars could not always be applied to current conflicts. The ability of the North Vietnamese and the Viet Cong to withstand repeated bombings and artillery attacks was surprising, and even the jungle terrain

Some experts believe that the overuse of advanced weaponry (such as helicopters) actually hindered U.S. efforts in Vietnam.

proved itself a difficult aspect of war to master. The tactics that had held back huge waves of attacking Chinese soldiers in Korea did not work against the small-unit, ambush-style fighting that the Viet Cong favored. America had to rethink its strategies and continually learn from the Vietnam War as it unfolded.

Both sides indeed learned many lessons in Vietnam, but the cost of the curriculum came high. Although militarists may recall the Vietnam War as a huge test crucible for the latest developments in weaponry and techniques, more than a few Americans will remember it as the wrong war in the wrong place at the wrong time for the wrong reasons. Such was the Vietnam experience.

First In: The Special Forces

Outside of rifles and ordnance supplied to the South in the years directly before and after the 1954 partition of Vietnam, the first effective "weapons" America sent to the region were members of the U.S. Army Special Forces. These men served as advisors to the people of South Vietnam and trained resistance units to counter the growing infiltration of North Vietnamese agents and guerrilla fighters. Unwilling to send its army overseas, the United States instead intended to bolster the fighting power of South Vietnam's own forces in the hope that large-scale U.S. intervention could be avoided. By sending tens of thousands of Special Forces advisors, the Eisenhower and Kennedy administrations believed it would not be necessary to commit hundreds of thousands of combat troops to a war that could be as bloody and drawn out as the Korean conflict only a few years earlier.

The implementation of increased numbers of Special Forces in Vietnam was the brainchild of President John F. Kennedy and his advisors. The president had been impressed with the demeanor of these elite combat troops and deemed them aptly suited to keep a positive American global presence in regions threatened by communism. On June 15, 1961, Kennedy authorized the expansion of the Special Forces by three thousand men and gave them permission to don green berets as a signal of their elite status. Under his administration, the Green Berets, as these units would be called, expanded their ranks to over ten thousand members. Kennedy and his chiefs of staff also gave the corps new duties. Where once the Special Forces of the Eisenhower and previous administrations had been confined to organizing resistance behind enemy lines, they were now trained as counterinsurgents. In other words, they were given powers to combat any political or military operation intended to incite civil unrest in friendly nations.

President John F. Kennedy hoped that by sending in Special Forces, such as the Green Berets, the United States could avoid having to commit large numbers of troops to Vietnam.

The Viet Cong

South Vietnam was already plagued by insurgent (rebel) forces by the time Kennedy took office in 1961. The Vietminh army of Ho Chi Minh, which expelled the French from Vietnam and brought about the partition of the nation into the communist North and democratic South, was still determined to unite the nation under the banner of communism. Although many of the Vietminh returned to the North after the 1954 Geneva Conference that determined the border, the communists left five thousand to ten thousand soldiers behind to foment rebellion among South Vietnamese who shared the desire to oust the supposedly democratic government. In 1959, North Vietnam began directing the insurgents, now known as the Viet Cong (a shortened form of Viet Cong San, meaning Vietnamese communist), to initiate guerrilla action against the South Vietnamese government of Ngo Dinh Diem.

Well trained by years of fighting against French rule, the ex-Vietminh soldiers turned their citizen supporters into a clever and effective guerrilla army. Historians Michael Lee Lanning and Dan Cragg simply note the Viet Cong were "farmers by day and soldiers by night."[4] Weapons that had been cached from the previous conflict and others that had been smuggled down from the North were stored throughout South Vietnam, accessible on a moment's notice by the eager Viet Cong. Among these weapons were outdated but still deadly

American-made M-1 rifles and M-2 carbines as well as the new Russian AK-47 assault rifles. The AK-47 was a modern marvel. Supplied by Russian and Chinese communist agents, the AK-47 used a 7.62 mm round and could fire either a single shot or a spray of bullets if set on automatic. It was easy to repair and maintain and ideally suited to the punishing rigors of jungle fighting. With these weapons, the Viet Cong began offensive actions against military and civilian targets in South Vietnam soon after the Geneva Conference. Beginning as individual acts of terrorism—bombings, kidnapping, and murder—Viet Cong activity soon escalated to include cooperative ambushes and full-scale attacks on South Vietnamese installations.

The Viet Cong were supported in their efforts by the regulars of the North Vietnamese Army. Supplies came down from North Vietnam along an irregular series of

A Viet Cong guerrilla holds his AK-47. Well-suited for jungle warfare, the AK-47 was the weapon used by a majority of the Viet Cong.

roads and jungle paths known as the Ho Chi Minh Trail. This trail ran south along the Annamitique Mountains, twisted through Laos and Cambodia, and branched off in many directions to terminate in various strategic areas of the South. Thus well supplied, the Viet Cong worked in tandem with

Lacking adequate equipment, training, and motivation, the typical South Vietnamese soldier (pictured) was ineffective against the Viet Cong.

the NVA to attack South Vietnamese targets beginning in 1960. The Army of the Republic of Vietnam (ARVN)—South Vietnam's military—was often overwhelmed in these attacks. Its leaders were poorly trained, and many were not professional soldiers but local bureaucrats who were owed favors by Ngo Dinh Diem. The troops were equally lackluster, often forced into service or simply signing on to earn a wage. Their equipment was World War II vintage M-1 rifles; few automatic weapons were in South Vietnam's arsenal and many of those were kept close to Saigon, where Diem resided. With little fighting spirit and no experience in the guerrilla war the Viet Cong were waging, the South Vietnamese Army was in need of assistance.

Training the South Vietnamese

Since 1957, that assistance had come in the form of active training from American Special Forces advisors. Their major objectives were to instruct the ARVN troops in guerrilla warfare and to give them diplomatic tools to win over the local populations who were subject to the influences of Viet Cong propaganda. In one training exercise in 1957, Capt. Harry G. Cramer of the 14th Special Forces Detachment became the first American casualty of the conflict in Vietnam. Thereafter, temporary-duty teams from the 1st, 5th, and 7th Special Forces Groups appeared in Vietnam in increasing numbers. By the spring of 1962, some six thousand Americans were serving in South Vietnam. Many of them were Special Forces teams or detachments working under the auspices of the Central Intelligence Agency (CIA) (the U.S. Army was not yet officially involved) in the Central Highlands and in the northern region to enlist and train the diverse mountain tribes in the service of the Saigon government.

The Americans knew that they would have to curry favor with civilian populations if they were to win against guerrilla fighters who were equally determined to turn the public against Diem's regime. The National Liberation Front (NLF), the political wing of the Viet Cong, was very successful in gathering support for the communists. Diem was an American-influenced puppet leader and his government showed little interest in bettering the lives of the rural populations who had been struggling to survive by farming through decades of conflict. The NLF had no trouble convincing many farmers that the Saigon government would not rush to their aid. The Special Forces advisors had to find support among a population that was disinclined to remain loyal to Diem's so-called democracy.

The Kindred Montagnards

The Americans initially found that support—and their civilian army—not in the rural rice paddies in the deep south, but in the mountains and highlands surrounding them. Here, tribes of mountain people called Montagnards (a term held over from French rule) lived by hunting and farming. They were rather isolated and had suffered years of oppression by Vietnam's government. They distrusted the Vietnamese of the South because they were of Chinese ancestry, and the South Vietnamese in turn looked down on the Montagnards as barbarian, calling them *moi*, lowly savages.

The U.S. advisors took to these tribesmen at once. As combat veteran Hans Halberstadt observes, "The motto of Special Forces is *De Opresso Liber,* or *Free the Oppressed,* and it was pretty much love at first sight between these two communities."[5] Although some of the thirty-three or more different Montagnard tribes were influenced by the NLF, many were willing to follow the tough and capable American advisors. "Many of the Montagnards were warriors in the classic sense," write military historians James F. Dunnigan and Albert A. Nofi. "They literally laughed at death and got on very well with the warrior types attracted to U.S. Army Special Forces duty."[6] The Special Forces soldiers showed their commitment to the Montagnards by studying their tribal customs, learning their native dialects, eating their foods, and partaking of their tribal ceremonies. The bond of trust, mutual dependence, and fighting spirit that quickly formed between the Montagnards and Special Forces soldiers yielded a unique military organization.

The bond was strengthened by the fact that the Special Forces men were suitably trained to live the rugged life of the mountain people and therefore help wage a war of counterinsurgency. Shelby L. Stanton, a critically acclaimed military historian and former member of the Special Forces in Southeast Asia, explains:

> Unconventional warfare, by its very nature, demanded rugged individuals who were able to master critical military skills needed to train and lead guerrilla warriors, to be inserted anywhere in the world by any means of transportation, to survive the most hostile environment, and to take care of themselves and others under harsh combat conditions. At the same time, these individuals had to be independent thinkers; able to grasp opportunities and innovate with the materials at hand. In or-

The Mountain People

The Montagnards, an ethnic minority of diverse Mon-Khmer and Malayo-Polynesian peoples, occupied the rugged length of the Vietnamese western highlands. In *Green Berets at War*, former Special Forces officer Shelby L. Stanton, who once lived among the Montagnards, describes them this way:

> In Montagnard culture, village chieftains were elected by the people, sorcerers and shamans held exalted positions, and justice was meted out with alcohol payments for offenses and livestock fines for serious crimes. Disputes were settled by seeing which party became drunk first or which individual came to the surface first after being dunked in a stream. . . .
>
> Clothing usually consisted only of loincloths. Wealth was indicated by the colors and embroidery of the clothing, or the silver, brass, and glass-bead jewelry worn. Bahnar Montagnards traditionally filed their upper teeth in adolescence. The Montagnard loved alcohol and rice wine. The Raglai tribe stayed inebriated from December to April, following their harvest. . . . They were brave hunters and skilled in the use of poison. Meals included wild plants, roots, lizards, snakes, and rats.

The close ties Montagnard warriors developed with U.S. Special Forces allowed them to become effective fighting units.

der to control and lead irregular parti-san fighters, they had to understand people, languages, and foreign cultures. Most important, the Special Forces warriors had to possess the intelligence, knowledge, tact, and acumen to successfully transform ordinary civilians into an effective military threat to a strong and cunning occupation army.[7]

And the Montagnards, with a strong warrior tradition and a knowledge of survival in the rural areas of South Vietnam, were equally well suited to wage a guerrilla war.

Most important to the Americans, the Montagnard tribesmen were located in a strategically significant region. Former Special Forces colonel Rod Paschall recognized the Montagnards' advantage:

These hill tribesmen comprised only about a million of South Vietnam's population of 18 million. But it was where they lived that mattered, not their numbers. First, they occupied more than half of Vietnam's countryside. . . . Second, the hill tribesmen dominated the high plateau region of South Vietnam and that area was the prime strategic target of the communists.[8]

The Americans knew that if the Viet Cong succeeded in gaining control of the highlands in South Vietnam, they could cut the country in two, leaving the northern region isolated from supply and making coordinated military ventures difficult.

CIDG and SOG

To thwart that plan, U.S. advisors had begun forming the Montagnards into military units as early as December 1961. The strategy was to arm and train the tribesmen so that they could defend their villages against Viet Cong infiltration or attack. The Montagnard units were given the name "cidgees" after the acronym for their new title, the Civilian Irregular Defense Group (CIDG). When the program proved successful, CIDG training was broadened to include offensive strikes against Viet Cong patrols and camps. By 1963, 43,000 Montagnard militia (village defenders) and 18,000 Montagnard assault troops were enlisted in the CIDG program. The next year, the U.S. advisors had created twenty-one armed defensive CIDG camps along major Viet Cong access routes into the South, including the all-important Ho Chi Minh Trail.

In 1963, President Diem was killed in a coup by his own generals; a military government fully supported by the United States took charge. That same year, the CIA turned control of the Special Forces teams conducting offensive actions against the North Vietnamese over to the U.S. military. The U.S. government then promptly established the Special Operations Group (SOG) in the following year to declare an official American military presence in Vietnam. However, the command was quickly renamed Studies and Observation Group to mask its covert nature, since America was still not technically at war in Vietnam and because much of the action along the Ho Chi Minh Trail brought

Green Berets into parts of Laos and Cambodia, nations that would not sanction a U.S. presence within their borders.

The SOG strike teams along the Ho Chi Minh Trail were primarily made up of three Green Berets and six to nine Montagnard mercenaries who were willing (for pay) to conduct operations away from their villages and even across the Vietnam border. Some SOG teams even inducted Laotian mercenaries into their outfits when the opportunity presented itself. Most of these teams conducted reconnaissance missions, scouting out the locations of NVA camps along the trail. Once these teams went out on a mission, they were typically isolated from any support; therefore, most carried a full arsenal of weapons in case the chance arose to assault a lightly defended supply depot or simply to defend themselves in case the SOG team came under attack. Rod Macon, who served three tours of duty with SOG and was wounded three times, describes the preparations for a "recon" mission into Laos:

> After the briefing, we pulled our equipment and went over the operation in detail. Even though we would make every effort to avoid contact, we still went in loaded for bear. My personal weapons included a Swedish K submachine gun, a sawn-off 12-gauge shotgun shoved down the top of my rucksack with 24 rounds of 00 buckshot and ten "flechette" [dart-shaped shot] rounds, a Browning High Power [pis-

tol] and my Gerber fighting knife. I also carried two Claymores [mines], two pounds of C4 plastic explosives, six frag[mentation] and two concussion grenades, two white phos[phorus] grenades and two smoke grenades, plus a bundle of canteens.[9]

Many teams like Macon's were successful in locating and even harassing the enemy, but the SOG units were certainly not an army that could carry out large-scale actions against the Viet Cong or the NVA.

Heroic but Futile Efforts

The Green Berets who were still manning the CIDG defense programs were likewise recognizing their limited effectiveness. Because of the importance of supplying the Viet Cong via the routes threatened by the CIDG base camps, the NVA soon turned to eliminating the CIDG blockade. The NVA needed to open these supply corridors so their resolve was strong and their assaults were fierce. Rod Paschall describes one particularly vicious attack on the CIDG camp at Plei Mei, illustrating the escalating actions in the Central Highlands and the types of weapons employed in these conflicts:

> The attack was led by NVA sappers [demolition experts used to clear approaches to fortifications] carrying satchel charges [explosives] and bangalore torpedoes. The assault pioneers [sappers] rammed pipe sections filled with explosives [the bangalore torpe-

does] through the barrier wire and blasted it apart in a series of detonations that rocked the camp. Streams of tracer bullets etched red lines across the blackness close to the ground as bunkered machine guns furiously pumped grazing fire into the tangle of barbed wire and struggling soldiers. Tribal riflemen and Special Forces sergeants fired weapons so rapidly that the barrels glowed. Onrushing North Vietnamese infantry staggered and fell in writhing agony as they were pitched into the upchurned dirt.

The northwestern bunker shuddered under a direct 57-mm recoilless rifle hit at 0600, which partially destroyed the structure. Dazed and bloodied defenders, wounded by shell fragments and splinters, reinforced sagging timbers and hauled more ammunition to the smoking machine guns.[10]

Although the NVA forces at Plei Mei were eventually driven off, both the Montagnards and their advisors realized the CIDG program was not equipped to repel a full-scale invasion.

Despite their experience and their zeal, the SOG strike teams and the CIDG defense forces could not stop the infiltration of the Viet Cong into South Vietnam, nor could they significantly stanch the flow of supplies along the Ho Chi Minh Trail. However, the Special Forces units did exact a toll on the North Vietnamese and the Viet Cong. For

Companions in the Jungle

Fighting along the Ho Chi Minh Trail and elsewhere in the jungles of Southeast Asia was at its best pure misery, at its worst, hell on earth. In "A Mean Place to Fight," in Page and Pimlott's *Nam: The Vietnam Experience 1965–1975*, Leroy Thompson, a former special-missions officer in Vietnam, recalls:

> You could die in a minute if a snake like a krait bit you. When you walked around at night, a branch might pull the pin on one of your grenades.

> Training, and the fact that we operated in small groups, was our way of keeping the jungle neutral. Our job was to convince the enemy that the jungle was ready to bring death at any moment by setting ambushes. Our "Hunter-Killer" teams of six men set ambushes using Claymore antipersonnel mines, detonator cord and automatic weapons. Our fields of fire were set to sweep a trail, with Claymores primed to pulverize anyone in our killing zone. Our job was to inflict messy enemy casualties and then blend back into the jungle. . . .

> We moved through the jungle in single file—"ranger file"—to minimize the chances of hitting a booby trap. We avoided trails for the same reason, though it made movement far more difficult. Our pointman frequently carried a shotgun so that he could sweep the area in front of him should he walk into an enemy patrol or ambush. In some cases, we had sawn-off M79 grenade launchers clipped to our harness and loaded with cannister rounds. Fear and discomfort were our constant companions in the jungle.

every SOG Green Beret lost in operations in Laos, for example, the North Vietnamese lost an estimated 100 to 150 troops. These

Combat Bums

Col. David H. Hackworth (U.S. Army, retired), America's most decorated living soldier, contends that the United States might have won the Vietnam War had "combat bums" been allowed to run it. In his memoir *About Face*, written with Julie Sherman, Hackworth asserts:

> Combat bums came in two (albeit overlapping) varieties: those who would have marched to the sound of guns wherever they were blazing (and/or had become, as I had, obsessed with figuring out a way to win this particular conflict) and/or those

who'd gone native. The natives were most easily identifiable. These were guys, many from Special Forces, who'd been there so long that the place had become a way of life for them. They loved the food, they spoke the language, many owned digs [dwellings] in Saigon or one of the other cities, and had Viet girlfriends to go "home" to when they weren't playing war. Most proudly wore brass bracelets that looked as if they were made of welding rods; besides the occasional gold Buddha a guy wore around his neck, this was the one real outward display of combat-bum status, and proudly signified nothing less than honorary membership in a Montagnard tribe. As a body, almost by definition, the Special Forces in Vietnam were combat bums *and* the best guys to fight the G[uerrilla] in this war. But the Special Forces were also animals, which offended all the prancers [those who wanted to conduct a civilized war], and they considered themselves an elite force, which offended most everybody else. General [Creighton] Abrams [General Westmoreland's successor in 1968] *hated* them. Yet, if these Green Berets had been allowed to run the show, there's little doubt in my mind that the outcome of the war would have been quite different.

Colonel David H. Hackworth feels that had "combat bums" directed the Vietnam War, the outcome would have been different.

numbers attest to the combat efficiency of the men who wear Green Berets; so do the plaudits and respect of their foes. Nguyen Tuong Lai, a former NVA officer who served on the Ho Chi Minh Trail, later said that the Green Berets "effectively attacked and weakened our forces and hurt our morale because we could not stop these attacks. We understood that these American soldiers were very skillful and very brave in their tactics to disrupt infiltration from the North."[11] Another former NVA soldier told writer Al Santoli that SOG members were beyond question America's finest fighters of the war.

Meritorious Conduct

Special Forces units continued their actions when American combat troops were finally called in to aid in repelling the North Vietnamese invasion in 1965. The Special Forces men fought in twelve major campaigns throughout the war. Their covert activities and their reconnaissance missions successfully altered the course of several military operations. As former Green Beret Shelby L. Stanton writes, "The Special Forces performed a host of strategic intelligence-collecting missions which in many instances were of decisive importance to battles and campaigns."[12] For their duty, Green Berets earned seventeen Medals of Honor and eighty-eight Distinguished Services Crosses during the Vietnam War.

Their conduct and their battle record, however, did not save them from criticism. When President Richard Nixon started withdrawing American troops from Vietnam in 1969 in order to turn the responsibility for combat operations back over to the South Vietnamese, the Saigon government, looking for scapegoats for their failing military, blamed the Special Forces for encouraging Montagnard rebellion against Saigon authority. The ethnic strife between the Montagnards and the South Vietnamese grew so intense that without the Special Forces advisors leading the CIDG and SOG teams, many Montagnards defected to the North Vietnamese Army.

Of course, such desertion also speaks to the leadership abilities of the Green Berets and the respect that the mountain tribesmen accorded them. Regardless, by the end of the war nothing seemed capable of holding the South Vietnamese Army together. The efforts of the Special Forces were ultimately as inconsequential in keeping the communists from uniting their nation as all other attempts foreign and domestic. But the Special Forces' pride in their service was well deserved. Despite growing antiwar sentiment in the United States and a deteriorating military strategy overall, many Special Forces members cherish the experience. Will Curry, who operated out of SOG command and control headquarters in Kontum, in the northern Central Highlands, said years later, "If you had to sell parts of your life, the last piece I'd sell is the eighteen months I spent running recon at Kontum."[13] Will Curry among them, these elite soldiers earned worldwide respect for their tenure in Vietnam and the Special Forces retains its reputation to this day.

★ Chapter 2 ★

Overcoming the Jungle: The Ground War

The first U.S. regular troops to arrive in Vietnam came ashore via amphibious landing on March 8, 1965, at Da Nang, South Vietnam's second-largest city. The two marine battalions under Brig. Gen. Frederick J. Karch staged an elaborate beach landing despite the fact that the air base at Da Nang was in perfect working order and would have made the ferrying of troops easier and less costly. But it also would have made the arrival less dramatic. The amphibious landing was meant to send a message to North Vietnam and its Chinese and Soviet allies that America was unwilling to let South Vietnam fall to communist rule. "We've been ready to do this job for some time," General Karch commented. "There's a sense of relief at the prospect of getting some action."[14]

But no action came for the marines. Their immediate mission was to secure the air base and deploy for its defense. The marine helicopter squadrons that now perched on the runways of Da Nang were not given orders to seek out and strafe enemy positions; instead they were handed the inglorious task of flying cargo loads of livestock to hungry ARVN troops in the surrounding countryside. Peacefulness and inactivity characterized the operation, but few knew it was the calm before the storm. For several days, the marines suffered no casualties. Then, unexpectedly, two marines were killed by friendly fire during a routine night patrol. In hindsight, their deaths seem ominous. As retired marine colonel Joseph H. Alexander writes, "The first Marine casualties made headlines. No one—*no one*—could have predicted that these few casualties were only the vanguard of over 100,000 Marines to be killed or wounded in action in the filthy war that ensued."[15]

Unfamiliar Warfare

By the mid-1960s America in the twentieth century had come through two world wars and the Korean War. The U.S. military was extremely well equipped. Nearly all the weapons of the previous wars had been replaced by better, faster, more reliable ones. Automatic rifles replaced semiautomatic ones, jets replaced propeller aircraft, and helicopters were used extensively as gunships and to ferry troops into battle. The military was also tactically proficient. It had learned from previous engagements how to move and deploy troops quickly and how to use planes, tanks, and infantry in combined operations to achieve victory.

For all its advancements, however, the U.S. military would bog down in the jungles of Vietnam. It had learned how to fight set-piece (preplanned) battles in open terrain where armored vehicles and aircraft could always support advancing in-

fantry. But Vietnam was a jungle nation. Armor could rarely penetrate the underbrush and airplanes would never see their targets under the canopy of trees. The U.S. military knew how to take positions and hold them as the enemy retreated from one defensive line to the next. Yet the Viet Cong and NVA troops were elusive. They were a people's army that could attack and melt back into the wilderness or hide among rural villagers. The Viet Cong held no ground and had no fixed positions to take. They moved freely in front of and behind American lines. Simply to fight the

The first U.S. combat troops arrived in Vietnam during an amphibious landing at Da Nang, March 8, 1965.

Johnson Takes Over

On November 2, 1963, a group of South Vietnamese military officers overthrew the government of Ngo Dinh Diem in Saigon and assassinated Diem and his brother Nhu. Because of Diem's failure to cope with civil disunity in the face of the growing communist challenge in South Vietnam, his regime had lost favor with the United States. Consequently, many sources suggest that the United States tacitly approved the coup. A military triumvirate (three-person government)—formally headed by former vice president Nguyen Ngoc Tho but dominated by Gen. Duong Van Minh—replaced Diem. (The South Vietnamese leadership subsequently passed, in bloodless coups, first to Maj. Gen. Nguyen Khanh in January 1964, and then to Maj. Gen. Nguyen Van Thieu in June 1965.) Twenty days after Diem's assassination, U.S. president John F. Kennedy suffered a similar fate in Dallas. The situation in South Vietnam continued to deteriorate under Minh and his successors. And the problem of U.S. involvement in Vietnam that had begun during the Truman administration now belonged to President Lyndon Baines Johnson.

Lyndon B. Johnson took over as U.S. president after the assassination of John F. Kennedy.

war, let alone win it, American strategists had to overcome their weaknesses and adapt to a type of guerrilla warfare that was totally alien to their training.

Before the U.S. military could develop a "jungle strategy," however, the generals had to know American troops would be utilized in the war.

Initially, American commitment to the ground war was minimal and President Lyndon Johnson, who took office in November 1963 when Kennedy was assassinated, wanted it to remain that way. All efforts were focused on training the South Vietnamese Army to successfully defend the country. But it was evident early on that the ARVN forces were not strong enough, so Johnson reluctantly agreed to send more troops. By May 1965, fifty-thousand U.S. combat troops were in Vietnam. Still, Johnson wanted the U.S. military strategists to wage a minimal war, one that would keep U.S. casualties low and show that the troops were there only to support the ARVN, not fight the war for them. Gen. William C. Westmoreland, commander of the U.S. troops in Vietnam, was thus asked to fight a war with one hand tied behind his back. He felt that full commitment could win the war, but given Washington's directives, he was bound to fight with restrictions.

Maxwell Taylor, a veteran commander of World War II and U.S. ambassador to South Vietnam under Johnson, suggested a strategy to the president that might minimize U.S. involvement. He advocated that the military adopt an "enclave strategy" that would fortify positions around key targets in South Vietnam. From these positions U.S. patrols could operate, but the relative safety of these positions would keep the bulk of the U.S. forces protected. Westmoreland disagreed with the plan, seeing that fixed positions would be ineffective against the guerrilla army that was building throughout South Vietnam. Johnson, however, agreed with Taylor and authorized Westmoreland to conduct operations only within a fifty-mile radius of any enclave and, furthermore, to commit U.S. military muscle only "to strengthen the relative position"[16] of ARVN forces in the field. Going against the spirit of Johnson's directive, Westmoreland used the latter part of the order to justify America's first large-scale operation of the war.

Initial Strategies

On June 27, 1965 an eight-battalion force of American, South Vietnamese, and some Australian and New Zealand allied troops launched a raid into a Viet Cong stronghold known as War Zone D, near the U.S. air base at Bien Hoa, northwest of Saigon. The joint foray produced several sharp engagements and may have forestalled a Viet Cong attack on the base, but results were inconclusive. Westmoreland, however, pointed to the effectiveness of the U.S. action and used the raid as an opportunity to request more American troops to bring resolution to the conflict.

Johnson, faced with an American public that was hoping he would adhere to his promises of minimizing U.S. commitment, reluctantly agreed to the request only after Secretary of Defense Robert S. McNamara and Henry Cabot Lodge (who replaced Maxwell Taylor as ambassador) recommended that he do so. But his commitment was still cautious. Westmoreland wanted 175,000 men immediately; he got 50,000 with the statement that more could be requested later. U.S. troop strength went up to 125,000 in Vietnam, and Johnson's approval rating at home went down.

With fresh troops, Westmoreland put into action his strategy of using American soldiers on the offensive. In August 1965, intelligence reports indicated that a Viet Cong regiment had entrenched itself on the Van Tuong Peninsula, only fifteen miles south of the marine airstrip at Chu Lai. Westmoreland seized the chance to show what his marines could accomplish if given the go-ahead to act aggressively. Code-named Operation Starlite, the American plan was to combine a land, sea, and air assault on the Viet Cong position and trap the enemy on the peninsula. In a superb demonstration of mobility and fighting efficiency, the marines destroyed the Viet Cong regiment, killing 614 enemy troops while suffering only 45 casualties.

Westmoreland's strategy had worked; he found the enemy through reconnaissance and then pulled in enough force to eliminate them. This strategy of "search and destroy" was repeated over and over in the American offensive. The Americans had learned how to crush the enemy, but the Viet Cong also limped away with a valuable lesson: Never stand ground for any length of time against the Americans. As marine historian Joseph H. Alexander notes, "Never again would a Viet Cong force offer pitched battle against Marine regiments."[17] The North Vietnamese Army learned a similar lesson at Ia Drang in November. Nearly three thousand NVA troops were staged against a smaller U.S. force, but the Americans had rocket artillery, close support helicopter gunships, and air cover from massive B-52 bombers. With well-coordinated attacks, the NVA were beaten off and fled into Cambodia, leaving more than twenty-five hundred casualties behind.

The communists learned to rely on hit-and-run ambushes that could cripple and confuse the Americans; their strategy entailed striking quickly and dispersing back into the jungle before the Americans could call in air support or bring a larger force to bear. They had to believe that their persistence and patience would wear down the American troops or at least wear down an American public that was not eager to wage a prolonged conflict in which the death toll of U.S. soldiers was broadcast nightly on television.

The American Platoon in Combat

The strategic part of the war would go on this way until the end. The U.S. military would try to corner the Viet Cong or NVA and crush them before they could get out of the trap. In fact, though the United States eventually lost the war, the army won every major engagement it fought. But much of the fighting that went on in Vietnam was not during a major offensive. Many of the firefights that occurred were small platoon-level engagements involving fewer than a hundred soldiers. Typically these were encounters between the enemy and patrolling units sent into the jungle to locate them. U.S. long-range patrols were well-equipped, self-sufficient platoons that often ventured several kilometers into the countryside in search of Viet Cong. These men were isolated from ground support (though they could usually call in air support or helicopter gunships, and often did when enemy contact was made) and were subject to clever ambushes by the Viet Cong guerrillas. In these instances, only training, wits, and trust in his weapons kept the U.S. foot soldier alive.

The U.S. combat platoon in Vietnam was a unique fighting unit. Every platoon member had a dedicated task, for example, rifleman, machine gunner, tank destroyer, or grenadier. Subdivided into squads, platoon members were taught to fight as a team, using various weapons in concert to overcome or repel an enemy force. Their equipment was a far cry from that of the squads of World War II, which could never be sure if they would have a machine gun or any antitank weapons.

Perhaps the most powerful weapon the American platoon possessed was the M-60 machine gun. Firing a large 7.62-mm round,

Twin Victories

The Americans won an unprecedented victory at Ia Drang, but so, too, did the North Vietnamese. In *About Face*, David H. Hackworth, America's most decorated living soldier, explains the significance of the battle in the Ia Drang Valley:

> The big question of Ia Drang was why the NVA stood its ground in the face of our awesome firepower, and allowed such diabolical casualties among its ranks. Indeed, a significant part of the high-level American ecstasy after Ia Drang was its "proof" of the suitability of a war of attrition (the style of war General Westmoreland was waging) [a gradual depletion of the enemy's forces] in Vietnam. But while Westy opined that the reason the NVA stood was to protect a new supply and staging base in the mountains above Ia Drang, it was John Paul Vann [army lieutenant colonel and later civilian advisor in Vietnam] who correctly suggested that the NVA's purpose at Ia Drang—and hang the expense in lives—was to figure out how to beat the Americans' incredible firepower and amazing mobility. And they accomplished their mission. Sure, they were knocked on their [backsides] and took a long time to recover, and they had to cut back on their fledgling "Stage Three" set-piece [carefully preplanned] battles and return to "Stage Two" guerrilla hit-and-run operations. But from the fight they also learned to "hug the belt" of their enemy, to come in as close as they could in order to neutralize the killing power of our artillery and air support. At Ia Drang, the North Vietnamese *learned how to fight us*. And looked at in this way, even if the battle was an unprecedented victory for the Americans in our war of attrition, it was an equally unprecedented victory for our enemy in their protracted guerrilla war.

Two soldiers leap from a helicopter into battle. The North Vietnamese had to find a way to beat the Americans' incredible mobility.

the M-60 was a belt-fed, gas-operated, air-cooled machine gun that could lay down a solid base of fire at up to twelve hundred yards. The Viet Cong and NVA units had lighter Soviet-made machine guns with shorter range and they possessed heavier, clumsier machine guns that could outdistance the M-60, but the American weapon proved better overall in terms of portability and power.

Another area weapon the U.S. platoon carried was the M-79 grenade launcher. A snap-open shotgun-type weapon, the M-79 could fire a 40-mm grenade cartridge at a rate of five to seven rounds per minute and over a distance of 375 yards. The grenades exploded on impact and sent shrapnel up to five yards in all directions. An experienced grenadier could hit a target up to 200 yards away without even using the

weapon's gun sight. Of course, almost every soldier also carried hand grenades to add to the explosive power of the platoon. These included fragmentation grenades and white phosphorous grenades, the latter of which covered the impact area with phosphorous powder that burned everything it touched.

Although grenades had explosive power, rarely could they demolish the fortified positions of the enemy. That job was given to the M-72 light antitank weapon (LAW). Designed to eliminate enemy armor, the LAW rarely saw that application because the North Vietnamese possessed few tanks (as the Americans learned, armor was too unwieldy in the jungle terrain). Instead, American platoons carried M-72s to knock out Viet Cong bunkers. The LAW was a telescoping tube that, when extended, fired a high-explosive rocket. Unlike the vintage bazooka, which required two men to load and fire, the M-72 was com-

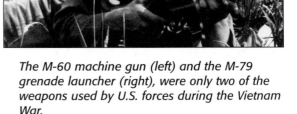

The M-60 machine gun (left) and the M-79 grenade launcher (right), were only two of the weapons used by U.S. forces during the Vietnam War.

pact and lightweight, measuring just over two feet and weighing under five pounds, and could be carried and operated by one soldier. The rocket was carried within the tube and therefore the weapon did not have to be loaded; yet once fired the LAW could not be used again. It was therefore a disposable weapon, and platoons typically carried several M-72 launchers.

The Amazing M-16

Despite the awesome firepower of the aforementioned weapons, the firearm used most frequently in the American platoon was the M-16 automatic rifle. The M-16 made its debut in the Vietnam War and proved itself a rugged and capable weapon. Unlike its eight-round, clip-fed predecessor M-1 Garand, which was carried across the battlefields of World War II and the Korean War, the M-16 was magazine fed—all of its twenty cartridges were contained in a detachable box clip that was shoved into the weapon—leaving the rifle otherwise completely enclosed. This novelty was meant to keep the action of the weapon free from dirt and the elements so that it could be counted on to fire even under the worst battlefield conditions. Yet when the M-16 first appeared in Vietnam, it became notorious for jamming. Dust went in the barrel and fouled up the firing mechanism, and because the weapon was enclosed, the only way to clear the obstruction was by forcibly ramming a cleaning rod down the barrel in order to push back the action. Of the early models, one marine wrote:

> Our M-16s aren't worth much. If there's dust in them, they will jam. Half of us don't have cleaning rods to unjam them. Out of forty rounds I've fired, my rifle jammed about ten times. I pack as many grenades as I can plus bayonet and K bar (jungle knife) so I'll have something to fight with.[18]

Despite its initial kinks, the M-16 rifle came to be the most widely used weapon in the U.S. arsenal.

When the kinks in the M-16 were worked out, the weapon served the foot soldier well. It was a light weapon, weighing under eight pounds, and small enough to be carried though the jungle terrain with ease. It was also made entirely of aluminum and plastic, which accounted for its lightness and it ability to stand up well to the weather. Rifles with wooden stocks often swelled in the heat and moisture, sometimes throwing off the firearm's sighting device. The M-16 remained unwarped in the jungle humidity and thus retained its accuracy. A 1967 *Newsweek* magazine report praised the M-16 as a major advance in small arms weaponry, describing it as "light enough to lug through the thickest underbrush, fast enough to spray 700 rounds of .22-caliber [5.56-mm] bullets a minute, and powerful enough to tear off a foe's arm at 100 yards."[19]

Adopting Guerrilla Tactics

Even given the powerful weaponry available to the standard platoon, the American forces were still handicapped in Vietnam. The Viet Cong knew the jungle well; they were familiar with aboveground paths and they had dug miles of underground tunnels that ran below many of the battlefields. Because they could not withstand a prolonged firefight with U.S. troops who could call in air support quickly, the Viet Cong relied on ambush tactics, and when they feared reprisal, they simply disappeared back into the jungle. This strategy typically inflicted a few casualties and left the remaining American platoon members powerless to exact vengeance. This helplessness, coupled with a feeling that the Viet Cong were everywhere and nowhere, unnerved many American servicemen. Furthermore, the Viet Cong were masters of concocting booby traps, which made their presence felt even when they were far away from the search radius of an American platoon.

Occasionally, the pent-up anger of the American troops was unleashed in blind fury in which vengeance was exacted on anyone Vietnamese. U.S. soldiers sometimes murdered innocent villagers in reprisal or by legitimately mistaking them for Viet Cong; at other times, entire villages were burned to the ground to "save" them from the Viet Cong. Of course, such actions did not endear the U.S. soldiers to the Vietnamese citizens and turned many to the Viet Cong cause.

More often, the U.S. combat soldier simply adopted the methods of the Viet Cong, creating ambushes and laying booby traps. In both instances, American platoons employed the deadly M18A1 Claymore mine with startling efficiency. The Claymore was a small antipersonnel mine that sprayed seven hundred steel balls up to fifty meters outward in a sixty-degree arc. Unlike other mines that are buried underground and set off by pressure, the Claymores were set aboveground at knee or ankle level and triggered by a trip wire or, more commonly, by an observer with a remote control. Several Claymores were usually set up so that they covered an area with overlapping arcs. If enemy soldiers came near, the Americans would detonate the mines as a first line of attack or defense. The indiscriminate projectiles would cut through anything in their path, leaving dead or wounded Viet Cong for the American infantry to mop up.

An Unpopular War

The use of such tactics signaled that the American forces were adapting to the guerrilla warfare that had been the hallmark of the Viet Cong. This education, however, did not ensure an American victory. Despite winning the major battles against the Viet Cong and North Vietnamese, the U.S. troops were only holding their own in the day-to-day fights in the jungle. And the Vietnamese soldiers, who had long endured foreign domination, had the advantages of patience and a will to overcome on their side. They also had the support of many dissident villagers who were tired of Saigon's oppressive governments and foreign armies of occupation. Most other civilians also harbored such resentments even if they refrained from taking any stand in the war. The Americans, who often struggled to keep the Vietnamese people neutral , never gained their allegiance or assistance. The populace was, in general, so apathetic to the war (the nation had been embroiled in conflict for so long that most peasants and farmers were just struggling to survive) that many American troops often wondered why they were fighting to "save" such an ungrateful lot. American antiwar protests at

A U.S. soldier prepares a booby trap with a Claymore mine. Over time, U.S. forces began adopting the guerrilla tactics used by the Viet Cong.

home also indicated to the soldiers that even their own country was unsure if fighting this war against communism was worthwhile.

President Johnson felt the pressure of political division and vowed to continue to fight a defensive war only. This appeasement gained little sympathy from war protesters; it was directed more toward North Vietnam's Soviet and Chinese allies who might be looking for an excuse to send troops to aid the communists. However, the decision not to invade the North was militarily absurd; without destroying the North and its capability to fight, the war in South Vietnam could feasibly continue indefinitely. These policies crippled the

The "Grunt"

The infantry soldier or marine in Vietnam called himself a "grunt," after the sounds he made moving about in the jungle while loaded down with the essentials of staying alive. In *A Contagion of War,* authors Terrence Maitland and Peter McInerney describe how Corp. John Clancy, a typical U.S. soldier in Vietnam, readied himself for a four-day patrol:

> During that time he had to carry everything he needed to live and fight. He wore a steel helmet on his head, securing a camouflaged canvas cover on its outside with an elastic strap, and drew on a sleeveless flak jacket made of bulletproof nylon. Over his shoulder, Clancy wore a patrol harness—a

set of heavy-duty green canvas suspenders. From this he suspended a pistol belt to which he attached his basic fighting load: two ammunition pouches, two fragmentation grenades, a smoke grenade, a "K-bar," or fighting knife, and two plastic canteens. Next he slung two bandoliers of 100 M-60 machine-gun rounds from his shoulders in a heavy, metal "X." On top of this Clancy shouldered a rucksack stuffed with a poncho that served as a raincoat by day and half a tent shelter by night, four days' worth of C-rations, personal effects ranging from toothbrush to Tabasco sauce, and plenty of extra ammunition, including twenty M-16 magazines, M-79 rounds for the grenadier, and a claymore mine. Inside the top flap of the rucksack Clancy tied an entrenching tool—a collapsible shovel he used to dig foxholes or fill sandbags. In all Clancy was burdened by roughly seventy pounds of weight not his own. Rigged with a release strap that permitted him to drop the "ruck" instantly, sometimes he almost welcomed the enemy contact that let him drop his house off his back. In his right hand he carried an M-16 automatic rifle.

The majority of operations in Vietnam were undertaken by infantry soldiers, or "grunts."

U.S. effort on the ground and were felt directly or indirectly by the soldiers, many of whom were simply tired of fighting and were losing confidence in their leaders. The war would drag on through Johnson's administration and into the Nixon presidency. Finally, with a nation growing weary of inconclusive warfare, the United States began withdrawing troops in 1969. Although America maintained its commitment and staged several major campaigns in the 1970s, by 1973 all U.S. troops were withdrawn as the North Vietnamese overran the southern provinces.

Chapter 3

Mobility and Firepower: U.S. Support Weapons

S peed and firepower were the deciding factors in the outcome of most battles in Vietnam. The U.S. military had an abundance of support vehicles—tanks, artillery, armored personnel carriers, and helicopters—that provided troops with lightning mobility and awesome firepower. Helicopters, by ferrying troops quickly into and out of any combat zone, became the hallmark of America's strategy of bringing the greatest force to bear upon the enemy. But fire support from artillery and tanks also figured predominantly into that design. Though these weapons could not normally advance through the jungle with combat soldiers, they could fire indirectly, raining high-explosive shells on a target designated by radiomen in the field. Tanks, of course, could also engage enemy soldiers directly in open terrain, and since the North Vietnamese Army had little armor initially, American firepower was usually overwhelming. All in all, these support weapons

gave the Americans and their allies a decisive edge that often turned the tide of battle in their favor.

Artillery and the Fire Support Base

In terms of artillery, the American forces definitely possessed the advantage. They had far more guns of usually higher caliber than the North Vietnamese; the Viet Cong typically had no field pieces at all. But warfare in Vietnam called for a change in the way artillery was employed. The new mobility of ground forces, engendered chiefly by the helicopter, created an ever-shifting battlefront. Without fixed front lines, a new way of providing infantry with artillery support had to be devised. Thus, air mobility and frontline fluidity gave rise to one of the most important American innovations of the war: the fire support base, or FSB.

The typical fire support base was a self-contained, self-defended artillery base from which infantry operations—particularly search-and-destroy missions—could be supported. Infantry units always operated within range of the FSB, whose support was always on call, responsive, and wholly reliable (unlike air support, which was limited by darkness and inclement weather conditions). In high-danger areas, infantry units were assigned to the FSB to provide additional security.

Fire support bases were always established within range of other FSBs for their mutual protection. The construction of FSBs held close to a set procedure, as summarized here by military historian David Miller:

The constantly shifting nature of combat during the Vietnam War led to artillery being used in new ways.

After reconnaissance and site selection, a stake was positioned at the center of the chosen site and a 131-ft (40-m) rope was used to mark [circumscribe] the bunker line. This [circular] line was marked by stakes at 15-ft intervals to indicate the infantry bunker positions. A circle of 246-ft (75-m) radius marked the line of the perimeter wire [although a perfect circle was seldom achieved because of variations in terrain]. At each bunker stake helicopters dropped a standard pack of one shaped demolition charge, two sheets of pierced steel planking, and empty sandbags, which were used to construct a 9-ft (2.7-m) bunker. Bulldozers excavated ground for the command post and fire support coordination center, and pits for the guns and mortars. A prefabricated 20-ft (6-m) observation tower was flown in by a CH-47 Chinook helicopter. Time of construction varied—but

Fire Support Bases, or FSBs, provided reliable and accurate artillery support for infantry units.

it was essential that the outer defenses and infantry positions were completed by last light on the first day of occupation of the FSB site.[20]

A typical, well-established fire support base might contain two triple M101A1 105-mm light howitzer emplacements and two twin 81-mm mortar emplacements (to fire high-explosive rounds or illumination flares to light up the compound and surrounding area during enemy night attacks). Also available onsite for defense of the FSB were night observation devices, Claymore mines, and the usual array of infantry weaponry—rifles, grenade launchers, recoilless rifles, and more. Helicopter and fixed-wing gunships, always on call, added colossal firepower when needed, as

did tactical air support, when flying conditions permitted.

The M101A1 howitzer is a rugged weapon that is easily transportable. Thousands of them saw service in Vietnam, used extensively by both the American army and the forces of South Vietnam. The gun's range is roughly seven miles, so infantry drawing support from the FSB had an impressive operational range. Yet by the same token, reliance on the FSB limited what the American infantry could do. In essence, they could not undertake a major offensive that would put them out of the range of the FSB support. Or perhaps it is more accurate

Artillery Battery at Work

In *America Takes Over 1965–1967,* military historians Edward Doyle and Samuel Lipsman assert that "the king of ground artillery in Vietnam was the 105-mm howitzer." They go on to explain how it is targeted in a combat situation:

> With a range of nearly ten miles, the howitzer could be brought to bear in a battle without actually being in the battle. This required sophisticated coordination between the battlefield leader and the artillery battery. The leader had to determine his exact location and the relative location of the enemy to his own location. He would then communicate the geographical coordinates to the battery. Since this knowledge was seldom accurate within 200 yards or so, artillery would first be called in to a point one felt certain was *not* the field officer's position. After seeing or hearing the shells strike, the target area would gradually be adjusted until it "found" the enemy position, a process that could take as little as five minutes or as much as thirty or more.
>
> A related problem was inaccuracy. Generally a series of shells fired at a single point from one gun would fall within about 50 yards of each other, but the pattern was elliptical rather than circular, offering advantages and disadvantages. Howitzers were more accurate with respect to direction than to range, so few shells fell to the left or right of the target, but many would fall long or short. Thus the relative position of the friendly and enemy forces played an important role in when and how the howitzer could be used. As with most weapons systems, the human factor—the judgment and talent of the field leader—was crucial in determining the usefulness of the weapon.

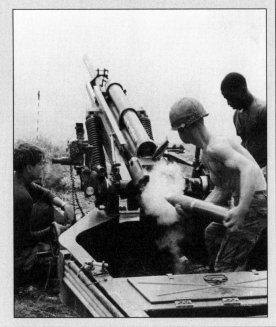

The 105-mm howitzer was the principal artillery weapon used in Vietnam.

to say that political and military leaders did not wish to risk the higher rate of American casualties that might result from fighting outside of the FSB's artillery range.

Although the NVA and Viet Cong were often crippled by the sheer firepower of the fire support bases, they did adopt new tactics in response to the threat. First of all, the North Vietnamese often targeted these bases for attack, and some of the fiercest fighting took place in and around FSBs. At Khe Sanh near the Laotian border, the marine garrison of the American firebase was virtually cut off (except by air) and under siege for the last few months of 1967. Only troops airlifted into the region and intense aerial bombings kept the base from falling to the waves of North Vietnamese troops. The second tactic the North Vietnamese used was what combat veteran David H. Hackworth terms "hugging the belt" of the Americans: "To come in as close as they could in order to neutralize the killing power of our artillery and air support."[21] By engaging the Americans at close range, the NVA and Viet Cong hoped—often in vain —that the U.S. officers would not call in fire support that might end up inflicting casualties on their own troops.

The Limited Role of Armor

For close support firepower, the Americans often relied on their tanks, though the terrain often negated their efficient use. The tanks' prime function was in clearing the major roads of the Viet Cong. Keeping these supply routes and communication arteries open was vital to the defense of South Vietnam, allowing the rapid movement of troops, ordnance, ammunition, medicine, and other supplies between key cities and strategic bases. As noted by John Pimlott, deputy head of the War Studies Department at the Royal Military Academy, Sandhurst (Britain's equivalent of the U.S. Military Academy at West Point):

As early as 1965, armored vehicles were employed to conduct all-day (or all-night) road marches between key points, laying down machine gun or

cannon fire along the roadsides to trigger potential ambushes or deter the VC from operating. These journeys were known as "Thunder Runs" and, although expensive in terms of ammunition, were successful."[22]

Of course, tanks were also used in direct confrontations with the enemy. By 1972 the NVA did possess some armor, primarily Soviet-made T-54s and T-55s, and as the war dragged on, their tank arsenal grew. The American and ARVN forces relied on the M-48 Patton tank to fend off North Vietnamese armored incursions, and despite its weaker-caliber gun (90-mm compared with the Russian 100-mm weapon), the Patton proved superior.

Even before the appearance of NVA tank forces, the Patton assisted the infantry in engaging the enemy. The M-48 excelled at destroying enemy bunkers with high-explosive rounds and caving in Viet Cong tunnels by its weight alone. A "flame-thrower" round introduced in 1968 gave the Patton added destructive potential; rather than actually spewing forth a jet of flame, the new round burst into flame on impact. But for all these capabilities the American tanks saw limited service in the dense jungle terrain they could not overcome.

Although the use of tanks was limited, another form of tracked vehicle was quite popular and effective in Vietnam. The M-113 armored personnel carrier (APC) was first issued to the South Vietnamese Army in 1963. Originally designed to ferry troops in and out of battle, the box-shaped hull was fully enclosed, protecting the eleven soldiers within from hostile small-arms fire. But the so-called battlefield taxis proved so versatile that thousands served ARVN and American forces. The APCs were watertight and weighed only 10.5 tons (compared to the 47 tons of the M-48 Patton), making them ideal for traversing the flooded rice paddies that dotted the Mekong Delta and other lowland combat zones. The standard M-113 also carried one .50-caliber and two 7.62-mm machine guns that were quite useful and potent in close-range firefights. Other variants carried mortars, flamethrowers, and even guided missiles, proving that the basic ve-

hicle was adaptable and easily converted. Yet, as with the tanks, the APCs were easily destroyed if the enemy could get close to the vehicles with antitank devices. The jungle terrain often made that possibility likely, and M-113s were rarely seen in or near densely overgrown regions.

Helicopters

Where tanks and armored personnel carriers could not operate, helicopters could. Perhaps no other weapon is as closely identified with the Vietnam War as the American heli-

Although it was ideal for traversing flooded rice paddies, the M-113 armored personnel carrier proved ineffective in dense jungle situations.

The Helicopter Paradox

The use of helicopters in the Vietnam War has been both widely applauded and criticized. In "Helicopters," part of *The Oxford Companion to American Military History*, authors Frederic A. Bergerson and Jason E. Trumpler assess the role of the helicopter in Vietnam:

> In 1965, the army and the air force reached an understanding in which responsibility for helicopter operations were assigned to the army. At approximately the same time the 11th Air Assault Division was redesignated the 1st Cavalry Division (Airmobile), and with its 16,000 troops and more than 400 helicopters was assigned to Vietnam. . . . In many respects the Vietnam War was a "helicopter war" and by 1970 the U.S. Army operated about 12,000 aircraft, the overwhelming majority of which were helicopters.

Helicopters provided American commanders in Vietnam a great deal of flexibility in their operations. They enabled the quick evacuation of wounded troops from the battlefield and saved thousands of lives, thereby holding the politically important death statistics down. Paradoxically, helicopters enabled U.S. troops to engage in combat in areas that otherwise would be inaccessible. The ability to land helicopters in any area with a small cleared space enabled the United States to establish bases known as LZs (landing zones), which produced a battlefield which distinctly lacked a clear demarcation between the friendly and enemy lines. The airmobile capability of helicopters created a more effective fighting force for Vietnam, but it also limited the imagination of tacticians who used this asset in cases where helicopters may not have been the wisest choice to employ. Nevertheless, the sound of helicopters became associated with the Vietnam War in the nightly news and motion pictures.

U.S. troops disembark from helicopters. The American use of helicopters in Vietnam has been both praised and criticized.

copter. Critics of the helicopter claim that it shaped U.S. strategy in Vietnam, meaning that the military relied so heavily on it that battle plans that did not incorporate air mobility may have been scrapped. Advocates of the rotary-winged aircraft, however, valued it highly. General Westmoreland, one of the helicopter's staunchest supporters, later wrote:

> We would have gotten nowhere in Vietnam if it hadn't been for the helicopter. Remember, along the borders of Cambodia and Laos we had a wide-open

flank more than seven hundred miles long, which we didn't have enough troops to defend. All we could do was lightly outpost the flank with Special Forces camps. Yet, when enemy units came across the border, we could use our helicopters to react with unprecedented mobility. If we'd had to move by ground, the enemy would have ambushed us constantly and we could have done little about it.[23]

How much the helicopter shaped U.S. strategy in Vietnam remains a topic for military authorities to debate. But one fact is undeniable: The U.S. experiment with helicopters in Vietnam profoundly impacted the art and practice of warfare.

Speed and Mobility

The helicopter, or "chopper," was first used successfully by the military in the Korean War, but it evolved in Vietnam. Several variants of the helicopter were widely used there, from the smaller dipper-shaped Bell UH-1 Iroquois (popularly known as the "Huey"), which served as a troop transport, medical evacuation vehicle, and fire support gunship, to the huge cargo-carrying Boeing-Vertol CH-47 Chinook, the workhorse of the American military. The helicopter gave the Americans and their allies unprecedented speed and allowed for rapid deployment of troops and supplies to any combat zone. Their trial by fire in Vietnam came in 1965 during the Ia Drang campaign. Gen. H. Norman Schwarzkopf,

who served two tours of duty in Vietnam and later earned fame as commander of U.S. and UN coalition forces during the Persian Gulf War, notes that during Ia Drang "helicopters were used for the first time to maneuver large American units in battle." As Schwarzkopf and others have concluded, "It was a landmark in modern warfare."[24]

As transports, Hueys basically served the same function as trucks: They moved soldiers to "hot spots," areas where Viet Cong and NVA were either fighting or massing for attack. Unlike trucks, however, the Hueys typically entered the battlefield; that is, they often dropped down to unload troops within range of the enemy. On the ground or at low levels, the Hueys were susceptible to small-arms fire or rocket attack. Their open sides—Hueys were designed without side doors to make unloading men easier—added to their vulnerability. The crew could defend themselves with machine guns mounted on both sides of the ship, but with men unloading in all directions, it was almost impossible to fire while on the ground without risking hitting the scrambling soldiers.

The Attack Helicopter

In the air, however, the helicopter was a valuable support weapon. In the early days of the war, Hueys, and even Chinooks, were fitted with a variety of add-on ordnance—machine guns, rockets, and the like—which made them a great threat. These ships could fly close to the ground fighting and, with the advantage of height, fire into enemy troops or alert the ground forces to the dangers ahead. In 1967 the role of attack helicopter was given to the newly introduced AH-1G Cobra. The smooth-lined Cobra was the first helicopter specifically designed as a gunship. Armed with a bow-mounted 40-mm grenade launcher and a minigun (a multibarreled rapid-firing machine gun) and wing-mounted machine guns and rockets, the Cobra presented a smaller target and delivered far greater fire-

The AH-1G Cobra gunship provided quick and deadly firepower that neither the Viet Cong or North Vietnamese Army could match.

power than its predecessors. A squadron of attack helicopters was extremely deadly. The aircraft would break up into teams of two and begin strafing ground targets at will. As ex-Cobra crewman John B. Morgan III explains:

Tactics were pretty simple. While one Cobra fired at the bad guys the other ship was going outbound on a racetrack pattern to position himself at a point where he could cover his partner's break and begin firing himself. . . . The front-seat man fired the turret and the back-seat man, usually the aircraft commander, fired the fixed wing stores and

flew the aircraft. . . . We usually got the job done even in marginal weather and at night.[25]

This firepower was typically enough to force attacking Viet Cong or NVA troops to retreat or at least bring them to a halt so that American or ARVN ground forces could recuperate and reorganize.

Attack helicopters alone flew almost 4 million sorties from 1966 to 1971, most of them in close support of ground operations. Helicopters of all sorts flew more than 36 million missions in Vietnam. Overall, the U.S. and ARVN helicopter squadrons lost more than 4,600 choppers. Military researcher B. G. Burkett and inves-

tigative reporter Glenna Whitley observe that a "study of helicopter casualties taken from the Vietnam casualty master computer tape" indicates that "almost 10 percent of those who died in Vietnam were killed in helicopter-related incidents."[26]

Fixed-Wing Gunships

Although the helicopter became in many ways the symbolic savior of American ground forces in Vietnam, other aircraft in the military arsenal were equally if not more effective in close-support operations. Perhaps even more threatening than the rotor noise of a low-level helicopter to the NVA and Viet Cong was the low hum of a twin-propeller AC-47 gunship. First appearing in

Attack on Fire Base Buell

Fire support bases represented enticing targets to the VC and NVA. In *After Tet,* Ronald H. Spector, who served with the marines in Vietnam and later as a historian at the U.S. Army Center of Military History, describes the communist attack against elements of the U.S. 25th Division at Fire Base Buell, near Tay Ninh, in August 1968:

> The Communist attack began at 1:00 A.M. with a barrage of 82-mm mortar fire. As the firing slackened illumination rounds from the 4.2-inch mortars revealed enemy forces advancing on the northern and southern ends of the base. The North Vietnamese mortar rounds hit an oil storage area near the 155-mm battery, starting a large fire, and two tanks were damaged by rocket powered grenades (RPGs) fired by a group of North Vietnamese soldiers who had managed to crawl forward through the wire on

> the northwest sector of the perimeter—but the base was never in danger. Deadly high explosive rounds called "Killer Junior" burst in the air above the attackers. As the North Vietnamese closed to under 100 yards, the gunners switched to rounds of "Beehive" canisters [filled with steel darts] fired at point-blank range. On the southern edge of the base, two Cobra helicopter gunships made repeated machine-gun attacks on the North Vietnamese, then were replaced by Air Force fighter-bombers and "Spooky" gunships, which remained on station throughout the battle. By 5:30 A.M. enemy fire had all but ceased. Most of the attackers had not even come within 10 meters [10.94 yards] of the wire. The Americans lost one dead and twenty-six wounded, while the Communists left 104 bodies and eight wounded on the battlefield.

the skies over Vietnam in 1964, the AC-47 Dragonship was basically a military conversion of the dependable Douglas DC-3 commercial airliner that had been around since 1936. Its propeller engines meant that it could travel at slower speeds than jet aircraft and therefore hover over battlefields, delivering sustained fire on enemy targets.

The AC-47 was originally pressed into military service as a C-47 transport plane, but in Vietnam it was armed to serve as a gunship. It possessed three multibarrel M-133 (gas-driven) or M-134 (electric-driven) 7.62-mm machine guns. Each gun could fire 6,000 rounds a minute. These Dragonships typically carried 24,000 rounds of ammunition and forty-five parachute flares with a burning time of three minutes each. Operating at night, they literally spewed fire and soon earned the nickname "Puff" among ground troopers. (The name derived from the pop song "Puff the Magic Dragon," popularized by the folk trio Peter, Paul, and Mary in the 1960s. Trio members reportedly shunned any association with the awesome killing machine.)

The Power of "Puff"

The AC-47 was also called "Spooky," after the nickname of the 4th Air Commando Squadron, the first air unit to fly them. Their eerie nocturnal light shows of flaming tracers and illuminating flares added to their ghostly illusion. B. G. Burkett, a lieutenant with the 199th Light Infantry in Vietnam in 1968, describes a typical "Puff" attack this way:

Occasionally "Puff the Magic Dragon" appeared to work its wicked sorcery. The Air Force had converted the venerable C-47 cargo plane into a hellacious weapons platform. Sporting several miniguns aimed out one side of the plane, the pilot flew in a circle around a target, putting thousands of rounds into enemy positions. Puff sounded like the whine of a mammoth buzz saw, and the streak of tracers made it look as if the "dragon" was belching flames. . . . I could only be thankful the enemy had no similar "dragons."[27]

The awesome firepower of the Dragonships' guns literally cut down anything in their path. Whole tree lines could topple as the "buzz saw" worked its way across the battlefield. Of course, the huge volume of fire ensured that any enemy troops caught in the blast were instantly dispatched. The AC-47s served well as deadly firing platforms, yet their main role was defensive. Unlike helicopters, which actively sought out enemy units, Dragonships were usually called on to aid hard-pressed ground troops. Many flew above base camps, keeping the tree lines free of enemy activity. Others were called into battlefields to help stem a Viet Cong or NVA attack, but because they expended their ammunition so quickly, they could not stay to provide prolonged assistance. Of course, by the time they emptied their ammo chests, the AC-47s had stopped the enemy cold, and helicopters or other support units would be called in to press a counterattack.

The Power but Not the Glory

The powerful support weapons in service with the American and ARVN forces turned the tide of many battles but failed to turn the tide of the war in Vietnam. In some cases, the inability of American tacticians to employ these weapons effectively in a jungle war kept such advanced technology from overcoming a peasant army. In other instances, political policy handicapped the military by defining the limits of U.S. aggression and restricting how and when American forces and their support weapons would be used in battle.

Despite the presence of artillery, helicopters, and tanks, much of the fighting in Vietnam was waged at close quarters by the common foot soldier. The dense jungle terrain would allow for no other option. More often than not, the support weapons were the saviors of the soldiers, on call once a battle began. In that role, they served their purpose well, either routing an attacking enemy force or extricating hard-pressed American or ARVN troops out of harm's way. Perhaps this is why the helicopter is so closely associated with the Vietnam War, for it could perform both functions admirably. Ironically, these battlefield saviors also became the symbols of America's withdrawal from Vietnam. In 1975, as NVA forces closed in on the South Vietnamese capital of Saigon, it was American helicopters that ferried American diplomats and lucky South Vietnamese civilians from the roof of the American embassy to American aircraft carriers offshore. And as the decks of the carriers filled with people, it was the helicopters—once proud symbol of America's fighting prowess—that were pushed overboard to make more room for the refugees from America's first military defeat.

Chapter 4

Rolling Thunder: The Air War

In 1964 incumbent President Lyndon Johnson won the presidential election against Republican challenger Barry Goldwater, largely on a campaign platform that opposed escalating the war in Vietnam. With only military advisors in the field, America's military presence there was minor, even though its orchestration of the defense of South Vietnam was holding the nation up. Johnson wanted to do no more than was necessary to keep the South Vietnamese Army on its feet fighting a defensive war. But this policy had left the U.S. military commanders flummoxed. Without the capability of launching invasions into the heartland of North Vietnam, the military was powerless to knock out the enemy's capability to make war. North Vietnam's industries and army training camps went undamaged, ensuring that the Hanoi (North Vietnamese) government could continue to arm and train soldiers to send south.

A turnabout in Johnson's policy, however, came early in 1965 when he appointed a National Security Council team to assess the progress of the war. That advisory team issued a report that declared that America's tactics were failing to oust the Viet Cong and had actually encouraged South Vietnamese to join the North's cause. In the first draft of its report to Johnson, the panel predicted that within six months to two years the president could likely expect the emergence of a "popular front government that will invite the US out"[28] of Vietnam. Johnson deliberated long and hard on the options the advisory team offered. He chose a "progressive squeeze and talk" strategy—that is, "a crescendo of additional military moves" against targets in North Vietnam and Laos (which had been harboring Viet Cong bases) alternating with offers to negotiate with the Hanoi government to reach agreement on terms for a "mutual withdrawal" from South Vietnam.[29] Johnson may have

Heavy fire from North Vietnamese antiaircraft guns became a constant threat to U.S. pilots.

believed that he was trying to force an honorable draw; to the American public, it seemed that he had broken his promise not to escalate the war.

Operation Rolling Thunder

Johnson adhered to his policy of not pushing the ground war north, so the main component of the "crescendo of military moves" was an American aerial campaign against North Vietnamese military bases and supply depots. The overall aim of the bombing campaign was to halt the flow of supplies from the North to the South and to force the North Vietnamese to the bar-gaining table by slowly exerting more and more pressure (or "squeeze") on North Vietnam. At the same time, care was to be exercised so as not to provoke either the Soviet Union or the People's Republic of China into intervening in the war (as China had done in the Korean War). Furthermore, Johnson considered these air strikes as defensive measures, punishment exacted in response to North Vietnamese aggression.

Code-named Rolling Thunder, the retribution bombing campaign began in February 1965 in response to Viet Cong attacks on U.S. bases at Pleiku and Qui Nhon in South Vietnam. The first target was an ammunition storage depot at Xom Bong, thirty-five miles north of the demilitarized zone (DMZ) that separated the two Vietnams. The raid consisted of 111 aircraft of various sorts that delivered 120 tons of bombs on the target area. On their return, pilots noted heavy antiaircraft fire along the flight path, and indeed, six aircraft did not return home. Five of those crews, however, were rescued by helicopters that located the downed airmen. The sixth plane's pilot, Lt. Hayden Lockhart, became the first U.S. Air Force (USAF) prisoner of war in Vietnam—the first of many to follow. Despite the losses, the attack on Xom Bong was a moderate success, and the U.S. high command was elated by the prospect of bringing the war to Hanoi.

The joy, however, was short-lived. The effectiveness of Rolling Thunder was curtailed from the start by Johnson's insistence on maintaining rigid control over the entire campaign. During his "slow squeeze" operation, no important target in North Vietnam could be attacked without permission from the president himself. "Hell, they can't even bomb an outhouse without my approval,"[30] Johnson quipped early in the campaign. From the White House Situation Room, nearly halfway around the world from the battlefront,

Johnson's targeting decisions were passed through Secretary of Defense McNamara to the Joint Chiefs of Staff and issued as directives to the commander in chief, Pacific, who apportioned targets and attack routes to U.S. and allied air units. This cumbersome chain of command frustrated and rankled commanders in the field. Johnson's tight control of Rolling Thunder not only produced an inflexible system that was incapable of reacting quickly to developing situations, but his restrictions on certain targets (such as those near the Chinese border) also created safety zones within which North Vietnamese assets remained free from attack.

Only in response to repeated warning that Rolling Thunder's effectiveness was compromised by the hamstringing did Johnson ease his restrictions. He authorized the use of napalm, an incendiary gasoline-jelly defoliant that destroyed huge swaths of a target area, and he allowed pilots to drop their bombs on alternate targets when the primary targets were obscured by weather or impenetrable because of enemy antiaircraft flak. In April, U.S. warplanes flew thirty-six hundred missions into North Vietnam, and it was evident that the retribution bombing was now a full-fledged campaign of destruction.

The Attack Planes

Operation Rolling Thunder provided a backdrop against which the air force, navy, and Marine Corps (for all three fielded planes during the campaign) displayed an intimidating array of aircraft that ranked among the finest in the world. Although some high-level bombers were used in the campaign (especially in dropping huge payloads along the Ho Chi Minh Trail), the bulk of the strategic attacks fell to the fighter-bombers and fighter planes. This was quite a change from the days of World War II, when waves of high-level bombers would saturate target areas with tons of explosives while fighter escort planes fended off enemy interceptors. By the Vietnam War, American technology had produced versatile aircraft—fighter planes could deliver bombs and missiles to targets as well as participate in air-to-air combat. A fighter's ability to pinpoint ground targets proved ideal to the conduct of the war in Vietnam for two reasons. First, the accuracy of missiles or small payloads of bombs meant that little collateral damage would occur, lessening the chance of civilian casualties. Johnson wanted to avoid the unnecessary slaughter of North Vietnamese civilians, fearing that saturation bombing of northern cities might prompt Chinese or Soviet aggression. Secondly, since much of North Vietnam's military targets were mobile— such as radar stations, supply trucks, and missile sights—pinpoint bombing, carried out by visual sighting of the enemy, meant a greater probability of hitting and destroying the intended targets.

To accomplish these feats of precision bombing, America primarily relied on three aircraft: the Republic F-105 Thunderchief, the McDonnell Douglas F-4 Phantom II, and the Chance-Vought F-8 Crusader.

The F-105 Thunderchief fighter-bomber, affectionately but sardonically referred to as the "Thud" (reputedly for the sound that it made when crashing) was the mainstay of USAF attack aircraft in the first half of the Vietnam War. It flew about 75 percent of all U.S. air strikes into North Vietnam during 1965–1968. At that time, the Thud was the heaviest single-seat jet in service, weighing 50,000 pounds. The F-105 was armed with one AIM-9 Sidewinder air-to-air missile and one internal M-61 20-mm Vulcan 6-barrel Gatling gun capable of firing 6,000 rounds a minute. It routinely carried four or five tons of bombs, which exceeded the bomb-load capacity of the huge, plodding Boeing B-17 Flying Fortress, the main Allied bomber of World War II.

"The name 'Thud' was an unfair call," writes retired air force colonel and renowned aviation historian Walter J. Boyne, "for the F-105 had a sculptural beauty" and "was a lovely aircraft to fly." It bore the brunt of the Rolling Thunder attacks and suffered heavy losses to antiaircraft fire and Soviet-built MiG fighters flown by North Vietnamese pilots. Of 833 original F-105 production aircraft, 350 were lost to combat or other operational causes. "Despite their relative lack of maneuverability and the manner in which they were employed [primarily as strike aircraft]," adds Boyne, "the F-105s managed to shoot down 27.5 MiGs often on the tail of another F-105 being attacked."[31] The F-105 engaged more

MiGs in air-to-air clashes than all other U.S. aircraft combined. Nearing obsolescence in the mid-1960s, the Thud was eventually replaced by the F-4 Phantom.

The Phantom and the Crusader

Most aviation authorities judge the McDonnell Douglas F-4 Phantom II air-superiority fighter to be the leading all-around combat aircraft of the 1960s. (An air-superiority fighter, as opposed to an interceptor, sought its enemies over hostile territory rather than engaging incoming raiders over home territory.) Though the plane was originally developed for the navy, the air force adopted the F-4 in 1962 for sixteen of the twenty-three squadrons then in its command. With a crew of two, it combined speed, range, agility, adaptability, ruggedness, and enormous firepower that went

unmatched until the advent of the Grumman F-14 Tomcat and other post-Vietnam-era aircraft. The F-4 carried powerful radar equipment and was originally armed with four Sidewinder and four AIM-9 Sparrow air-to-air, radar-guided missiles. An internal M61A1 20-mm Vulcan gun was added under the nose of the F-4E version.

The Chance-Vought F-8 Crusader joined the F-105 and the F-4 in participating in the bulk of the aerial strike missions and air-to-air fighting that took place over North Vietnam. Fast and agile, the Crusader was a single-seat, carrier-based, air-superiority fighter. It carried four 20-mm Colt Mark 12 cannon and two or four Sidewinder missiles

Carrying up to 5 tons of bombs, the F-105 Thunderchief flew the majority of the bombing missions during Operation Rolling Thunder.

Phantom Firepower

Designed as an interceptor, early models of the McDonnell Douglas F-4 Phantom II followed the then-current trend in armament and carried up to eight air-to-air missiles but no guns. The need for additional armament was recognized and a cannon was added later, much to the delight of pilots like Col. Robin Olds (as quoted by Norman Franks in *Aircraft Versus Aircraft*):

> Air-to-air missiles gave our fighters tremendous capability relative to the MiG-17, which carried only cannon and rockets. But fighting a MiG with a gunless F-4 is like fighting a guy with a dagger when he's got a sword, or maybe vice versa. A fighter without a gun, which is the most versatile air-to-air weapon, is like an airplane without a wing. Five or six times, when I had fired all my missiles, I might have been able to hit a MiG if I'd had cannon, because I was so close his motion was stopped in my gunsight.

When we got the General Electric Vulcan M-61, which fires 6000 20-mm shells a minute, it turned out to be the greatest gun ever built for a fighter. It jammed very little. One of our exceptional pilots, Captain Darrel Simmons, shot down two MiGs with this Gatling [Vulcan] in one day. He got them where he wanted them and just tapped the trigger twice for a total of 494 rounds. Of my 18 or more MiG scraps, the longest one was just 14 minutes. You have only a few seconds to fire in any MiG engagement, so I found our single Gatling's 6000 rounds per minute more than adequate.

The addition of a cannon to the F-4 Phantom made it deadly in air-to-air combat.

on "cheek" launchers attached to the fuselage. About half of navy fighter squadrons were equipped with Crusaders, which were flown by some of the best pilots in the world. Former USAF fighter pilot and Vietnam veteran Marshall L. Michel III states: "F-8 pilots were extremely well trained in maneuvering air combat—'dogfighting'—and were proud (some might say they were arrogant)

of their skill; they believed they and their aircraft were the best in the world in air-to-air combat."[32] American pilots found ample opportunities to test their aircraft and themselves in the MiG-contested skies over North Vietnam.

The Thunderchief, Phantom, and Crusader performed admirably in knocking out their given targets, but the ability of

North Vietnam to rebuild their losses and even hide their arsenals proved vexing to the U.S. high command. Also without saturation bombing of enemy population and industrial centers, the will of the North Vietnamese to continue the fight was not challenged. To counter this, America could only launch more and more air strikes, which Johnson grudgingly authorized.

Little Effect Against Stiff Resistance

The escalating air war also proved to be the pretext for bringing the first U.S. combat troops into the conflict. Fearing that the U.S. air base at Da Nang would be targeted by the NVA in retribution for the bombings, General Westmoreland requested the protection of U.S. Marines. A deployment of thirty-five hundred arrived in early March 1965. It became obvious that more and more American troops would be needed to limit North Vietnamese aggression since Rolling Thunder was failing to do so. A group of eminent scientists studied the statistical effects of the bombing campaign and issued a report in 1966 that concluded that Rolling Thunder "had not substantially affected the ability of North Vietnam to support the military operations in the South" and that "despite the bombing, the flow of aid from North to South had accelerated."[33]

Rolling Thunder was also taking its toll on the USAF. The North Vietnamese were certainly not defenseless, and American technology—though often superior—did not stand unopposed in the skies over Hanoi. The North Vietnamese air force was well supplied with Soviet-made MiG fighters that proved a match for the American pilots. The MiG-17 carried one 37-mm and two 23-mm cannon and later versions were equipped with Atoll air-to-air missiles, giving it substantial firepower. Although on paper the MiG-17 was inferior in performance and armament to its American

Fast and agile, the F-8 Crusader provided additional firepower during Operation Rolling Thunder.

Fighter Comparisons

The U.S. F-105 Thunderchief, F-4 Phantom, and F-8 Crusader fighters achieved maximum speeds at sea level of 730, 710, and 650 knots (nautical miles—1.15 statute miles—per hour), respectively. By comparison, the Soviet-built MiG-17, -19, and -21 fighters reached maximum respective speeds at sea level of 575, 595, and 620 knots. In *Clashes*, Marshall L. Michel III, a former USAF fighter pilot in Vietnam, examines some of the chief characteristics of these aerial adversaries:

> U.S. fighters were significantly larger (thus could be seen from a much greater distance) and also were three to five times heavier than the MiG-17 and from two to three times as heavy as the MiG-21. This was not, however, just dead weight—U.S. fighters had much greater range and more sophisticated electronics than the MiGs. . . .

The U.S. aircraft also carried more missiles and more cannon ammunition—for example, U.S. fighter cannon carried enough ammunition for about ten or eleven seconds of firing time, while MiGs carried enough for between five and six seconds, or about two firing passes. . . .

During Rolling Thunder there were two clear aircraft performance differences. The MiG-17 was inferior to all of the U.S. fighters and suffered losses that reflected that fact. Despite having excellent GCI [Ground Control Intercept; a ground-control radar system for controlling and vectoring friendly aircraft against hostile aircraft] and often attacking bomb-loaded U.S. aircraft, about eighty-seven MiG-17s were shot down, while they in turn shot down only twenty-three U.S. aircraft. On the other hand, the MiG-21 clearly was superior to the F-105: They shot down fifteen F-105s, while F-105s did not shoot down a single MiG-21. But with the F-8, F-4, and MiG-21, the differences in aircraft performance appeared to cancel each other out, with the outcome of a given battle depending on other factors.

The stiffest opposition encountered by U.S. pilots came from the MiG-21 fighter.

counterparts, U.S. pilots found it a worthy opponent. Col. Robin Olds, a World War II flying ace, downed two MiG-17s in his service in Vietnam, but still referred to the Russian fighter as "a vicious, vicious little beast."[34]

Other MiG planes were in service in the North Vietnamese air force, but perhaps the deadliest was the MiG-21 "Fishbed." Capable of Mach-2 speeds—more than twice the speed of sound—it exhibited excellent supersonic maneuverability and proved an able match for U.S. fighters. Armed with one 23-mm cannon and two Atoll missiles, the MiG-21s often lay in wait for incoming American planes and, with the help of spotters on the ground, coordinated attacks to pounce on the attackers and flee before they could be swarmed by the more numerous American fighters. Writes Walter J. Boyne:

> North Vietnamese ground control tactics used the MiG-21's capabilities perfectly, vectoring [guiding] them in pairs behind an incoming strike force. The Fishbeds would be positioned behind the formation, accelerate to supersonic speed, fire their heat-seeking Atoll missile, and zoom up and away from the strike force. Their mission was accomplished if they got the F-4s and F-105s to jettison [drop] their bomb loads [prematurely out of fright], but on too many occasions, the Atoll scored a victory.[35]

The MiG-21s were considered so dangerous that the U.S. military staged an operation to lure them into combat so they could be destroyed by superior American planes. The MiGs in question had been operating from air bases around Hanoi, and true to their tactics, had avoided dogfighting the American fighters in favor of ambushing the slower Thunderchief bombers. Gen. William W. Momyer devised a sweep of the air bases in an offensive code-named Operation Bolo. His plan was to conduct a routine bombing mission (one that the NVA had been accustomed to) over Hanoi, but to replace the Thunderchief bombers with F-4C Phantom fighters. He hoped the North Vietnamese, thinking the fighters were bombers, would send up the MiG-21s expecting to attack easy prey, and the Americans could finally dispatch the troublesome MiGs. In January 1967, Momyer's plan worked splendidly; within twelve minutes of aerial dueling, seven MiG-21s were shot down without the loss of any American fighters.

Flying Through Flak

The MiG fighters, however, were only one component of North Vietnam's air defenses. Radar-directed surface-to-air missiles (SAMs) constituted another element of the defense network. Radar-guided antiaircraft guns made up the third line. American planes possessed sophisticated electronic countermeasure (ECM) equipment to help foil the guided missiles by throwing off false electronic pulses that the enemy radar would mistakenly home in on, but the antiaircraft guns were not as easily fooled. Knowing the approximate area of the sky in which the American planes were located, the antiaircraft guns would throw up a barrage of flak in hopes of damaging anything within the target area. The technique was old, but with the

Smart Bombs

"To make a smart bomb," write Tim Page and John Pimlott, the editors of *Nam*, "you take the body of a dumb bomb and give it a brain." The so-called smart bombs have the ability to direct themselves to a target using laser beams, television cameras, computers, and infrared detectors. Page and Pimlott describe two such "brainy" bombs:

> The US Navy's Walleye glide-bomb was the first. It was a standard 850-lb high-explosive bomb with a TV camera in its nose. The camera could be used to lock the bomb into the target before it was dropped, then, using its tail fins, steer the bomb down its glidepath as it fell. . . .

> The problem was that locking the Walleye onto its target took about 15 seconds of straight and level flight before the pilot could drop the bomb and turn away. This

was a gift for the anti-aircraft gunners and Walleye-equipped aircraft suffered an average of four times as many hits from anti-aircraft fire as conventional "dumb" bombers. . . .

The US Air Force preferred laser-guided bombs (LGBs) to the Navy's electro-optical guidance systems, and they dropped some 25,000 Paveway LGBs during the war. First introduced in 1968, the Paveway made use of standard dumb bombs, to which a laser seeker unit and a steering wing assembly were added. The seeker unit detected light reflected off the target when it was illuminated by a laser designator. The bomb then steered itself onto the target with the rear-mounted fins. The laser target designator could be either ground-based or airborne. If it was airborne it could be mounted on the attack plane or another aircraft.

help of multiple radar installations giving the altitude and direction of the American planes, it was still effective. In fact, more American planes fell to antiaircraft guns than to fighters or SAM weaponry. Because of the potency of the antiaircraft weapons on the ground (including SAM bases), these installations were often primary targets of American bombing missions.

The End of Rolling Thunder

In the spring of 1967, Johnson ordered a further escalation of Rolling Thunder, authorizing the bombing of power plants, factories, and airfields near Hanoi. The campaign went on for another year, but the results were inconclusive. In March 1968, Johnson announced that he would restrict the bombing

of North Vietnam in pursuing a diplomatic resolution with Hanoi. He also announced that he would not seek reelection in November. Peace talks did commence in Paris but negotiations stalled in May. In an attempt to revitalize the talks, Johnson cancelled Rolling Thunder on October 31.

Over the nearly four years of Rolling Thunder, American planes flew 297,000 sorties and dropped 605,000 tons of bombs. The results were—as many conclude—insignificant. North Vietnam imported much of its war matériel from the USSR and China, and therefore few worthwhile strategic targets existed within the nation. The air attacks also failed to stop the flow of supplies down the Ho Chi Minh Trail. The North Vietnamese simply moved troops and supplies at night or chose paths other than the ones that were targeted for bombing. These tactics, coupled with Johnson's decision to limit the types and locations of targets that could be bombed, ensured that the overall effect on North Vietnam's war-making capability was not significant enough to alter the course of the war.

Nixon and the Linebacker Raids

In May 1972, Johnson's successor, Richard Nixon, reinstated the bombing campaign against the North. A massive NVA attack aimed at overrunning the South prompted Nixon to suspend peace talks and call for retribution. His renewed bombing campaign was code-named Linebacker I (after Nixon's own fondness for football). Unlike Johnson, Nixon had no intention of controlling the air campaign and designating which targets could be struck. He, therefore, removed most of the restrictions that had diluted Rolling Thunder.

Air force, navy, and marine pilots flew some 41,000 sorties over North Vietnam during the operation. Using high-level Boeing B-52 Stratobombers and navy mine-laying aircraft, as well as the usual wide array of U.S. fighter-bombers, American pilots mined North Vietnamese harbors, closing ports to oceangoing traffic, and destroyed ten MiG bases, six major power plants, and all of North Vietnam's large oil-storage facilities. These considerable accomplishments cost the loss of seventy-five U.S. aircraft, but the NVA drive was stopped cold. Almost immediately, peace talks resumed and in October,

as a gesture of good faith, President Nixon reduced Linebacker I activities to targets south of Hanoi.

The peace talks, however, broke down again late in the year. North Vietnamese diplomats stalled, and Nixon interpreted this as a delaying tactic to give NVA troops time to assemble for another big push. On December 18, Nixon ordered an all-out bombing campaign against Hanoi and surrounding regions. The assault lasted eleven days and became known as the Christmas bombings, but the official title was Linebacker II. Two hundred heavy B-52 bombers along with the typical fighter-bomber squadrons devastated North Vietnam's infrastructure. Many civilians were killed in the raids, and antiwar demonstrators in America discredited Nixon as a baby-killer, but ultimately North Vietnam did return to the bargaining table at the peace negotiations and signed the Paris Accords less than one month later.

Air power advocates point to the Linebacker campaigns as evidence that the war could have been won by the unrestricted use of air power alone. Critics, however, argue that the North Vietnamese would have agreed to the peace terms Nixon proposed in 1973 anyway because the terms were far more modest than those Johnson had demanded in 1965–1968. Whatever the case, the air war over Vietnam continues to attract controversy, but it is doubtless that the various campaigns—especially the Linebacker raids—helped bring about a resolution to a seemingly interminable war.

Chapter 5

Inland and Offshore: Naval Engagements

O n August 2, 1964, the American destroyer *Maddox*, on patrol in international waters in the Gulf of Tonkin off the coast of North Vietnam, was attacked by three North Vietnamese motor torpedo boats. The *Maddox*, aided by four F-8E Crusader fighter planes from the aircraft carrier *Ticonderoga*, repulsed the attackers. Navy officials reported one North Vietnamese boat sunk and two damaged. President Lyndon B. Johnson issued an immediate warning: "The United States Government expects that North Vietnam will be under no misapprehension as to the grave consequences which would inevitably result from any further unprovoked military action against United States forces."[36] Two days later, the *Maddox*, joined by the destroyer *C. Turner Joy*, reported a second attack by North Vietnamese torpedo boats.

According to the Pentagon Papers (official government memoranda documenting U.S. involvement in Vietnam from 1954 to 1968), U.S. intelligence officers later asserted that the "enemy vessels" identified in the second attack had in reality been radar "blips" caused by the wake of the *C. Turner Joy*. An inexperienced radar operator, reports reveal, had misinterpreted the blips. But Johnson, having been assured by his commanders in the field that an attack had taken place, believed that the North Vietnamese would consider further U.S. restraint as a sign of weakness. The president authorized an immediate retaliatory air strike on North Vietnam's torpedo boats and their bases. On August 5, he told the American public that the raids were in progress "as I speak to you tonight." And he repeated a theme that he had first expressed months earlier: "We still seek no wider war."[37]

Citing the two Gulf of Tonkin incidents, Johnson asked Congress for a resolution empowering him, in part, to "take all necessary measures to repel any armed attack against the forces of the United States."[38] Congress complied, enacting the so-called Tonkin Gulf Resolution (officially the Southeast Asia Resolution) on August 7. The measure passed by an overwhelming vote of 48 to 2 in the Senate and a unanimous voice vote of 416 to zero in the House of Representatives. Both Johnson and his successor, Richard Nixon, regarded the act as authorization to prosecute the war in Southeast Asia. Whether the second attack on U.S. ships in the Gulf of Tonkin ever actually occurred remains a matter of controversy to this day, but subsequent events in North Vietnam rendered a full-scale U.S. involvement in Vietnam little short of inevitable. And the naval war had already begun.

The Navy's Role

The role of the U.S. Navy in Vietnam was wide-ranging and diverse. Played out on the high seas, along the coast, in the air, and on the rivers, canals, and waterways, the naval commitment touched on every aspect of the Vietnam experience. From the task forces of the Seventh Fleet operating in the South China Sea to the river patrol boats that plied the inland waterways of Vietnam, the U.S. Navy participated in

A supposed North Vietnamese attack on the USS Maddox *and* C. Turner Joy *(pictured) led to the passage of the Gulf of Tonkin Resolution.*

many conflicts and helped shape the course of the war.

The Seventh Fleet was, perhaps, what most people imagine when thinking of U.S. naval involvement in Vietnam. It contained the battleships, cruisers, and aircraft carriers commonly associated with a modern navy. These ships were divided into task forces and given select tasks to perform. Task Force 77, America's attack carrier force, provided planes to carry out air strikes against North Vietnamese targets. Task Force 76 contained amphibious landing craft and was given the task of putting marines ashore wherever instructed. Task Force 70.8 provided naval gunfire support—from its many cruisers and destroyers—to soldiers fighting

inland. These various task forces assisted in major air and ground campaigns by using their huge guns as added artillery fire or, in the case of the carrier strike force, launching aircraft to carry out strike missions against designated targets.

Offshore Bombardment

The cruisers in Task Force 70.8 carried 8-inch guns and several cruisers and destroyers carried 5-inch guns. These weapons could devastate a target area. Neil Sheehan, an award-winning journalist who reported the

The 16-inch guns on the USS New Jersey *provided deadly offshore support to various operations in North Vietnam.*

Vietnam War for United Press International and the *New York Times*, saw firsthand the destructiveness of 5-inch shells in the coastal Bong Son Plain, in central South Vietnam. He noted that U.S. 1st Air Cavalry and ARVN airborne forces operating around Bong Son

> had drawn part of their fire support from Seventh Fleet destroyers. Naval shells are shot in a relatively flat trajectory. In just one of the hamlets I walked through along Route 1, hundreds of coconut trees had been snapped in half by the 5-inch projectiles.[39]

The task force operated primarily around the demilitarized zone. It was called into the conflict in May 1965, and in September of 1968, the battleship *New Jersey* was added to the group. The *New Jersey*'s 16-inch guns were even more powerful than the weaponry of the cruisers and destroyers. From 1968 to March 1969, the *New Jersey* fired off 3,615 of these huge shells in support of various operations along the DMZ. Task Force 70.8 was also called on to strike directly into the heart of North Vietnam during the Linebacker I air campaign in 1972. A cruiser and destroyer group pummeled coastal areas near Haiphong in support of the operation.

On Yankee Station

Also taking part in the Linebacker raids were the aircraft carriers of Task Force 77. On May 10, 1972, navy pilots flew 294 missions over North Vietnam from three carriers in the Gulf of Tonkin. These ranged from bombing strikes to dogfights with enemy MiGs. The navy pilots were so skilled that as Linebacker I progressed, they chalked up an impressive 12:1 win-loss ratio over their North Vietnamese counterparts. But these victories toward the end of the war were only part of the task force's story. The carrier group had been in operation all through the war, lending strike aircraft to the Rolling Thunder raids as well.

The carrier fleet operated primarily out of Yankee Station, a fixed rendezvous point in the Gulf of Tonkin. Three carriers were usually present in the task force at all times, although these were usually rotated in and out of service over several months. A total of nineteen carriers served as part of Task Force 77 during the course of war. Huge attack carriers such as *America, Constellation,* and *Independence* and even the navy's new nuclear-powered carrier *Enterprise* were among them. Their mission was not only to take part in major air campaigns, but also to assist ARVN and American ground forces as well as actively disrupt enemy supply lines.

A carrier wing on each "flattop" controlled from seventy to a hundred aircraft, usually grouped into two fighter and three attack squadrons and other detachments. The prime attack aircraft consisted of the Douglas A-1 Skyraider, the McDonnell Douglas A-4 Skyhawk, the Grumman A-6 Intruder, and the Vought A-7 Corsair II. Navy versions of the McDonnell Douglas F-4 Phantom II and the Vought F-8 Crusader

First Aces

On May 10, 1972, navy pilot Lt. Randall S. Cunningham and his radar intercept officer (RIO) Lt. (junior grade) William Driscoll shot down North Vietnam's top ace and two other MiGs to become the first American aces of the Vietnam War. Cunningham and Driscoll started the day with two kills to their credit: a MiG-21 on January 19 and a MiG-17 on May 8. As before, they used Sidewinder missiles in scoring their latest victories.

Their last air battle of the day pitted them against Colonel Tomb, leading North Vietnamese fighter pilot with thirteen U.S. aircraft to his credit. Cunningham maneuvered his F-4J Phantom against Tomb's MiG-17 for several minutes, as each pilot sought a firing advantage. Finally, as both aircraft climbed steeply, Cunningham throttled back and braked hard, causing Tomb to shoot past him. Tomb's MiG pitched earthward. Cunningham followed and released his missile. Tomb's MiG exploded and crashed into the ground.

Shortly after notching their third victory of the day, a surface-to-air missile caught up with their Phantom, but the Americans nursed their plane back over the Gulf of Tonkin before ejecting. A marine helicopter rescued both men and returned them to the attack carrier *Constellation*. Shortly after the war, Cunningham wrote a treatise called *Air-to-Air Tactics*. As reprinted in Mike Spick's *The Ace Factor*, Cunningham's paper began:

> The key to success in air-to-air combat is the pilot, his ability, training, and aggressiveness, with a little luck thrown in. You cannot enter the air thinking that you will lose. Personality characteristics have to be oriented toward the mission, and concentration directed to maximum performance. There are no points for second place. The pilot must have a three-dimensional sense of awareness and feel time, distance and relative motion as if they were part of his soul; only if you have a feeling for what is going on around you can you take action and make correct decisions. Analyzing multiple complex time and space oriented problems correctly is one significant key to aerial combat.

Cunningham (left) and Driscoll relax back aboard the USS Constellation *after becoming the first aces of the Vietnam War.*

doubled as strike and fighter-escort aircraft. With the exception of modifications needed for carrier operations, the Phantoms and Crusaders were essentially the same as those used by the air force.

Naval Aircraft

The Douglas A-1 Skyraider was a throwback to the Korean War era. Still, despite its maximum speed of only 318 mph in the age of supersonic aircraft, the lumbering, propeller-driven Skyraider served effectively in Vietnam. Armed with four 20-mm cannon, plus up to 8,000 pounds of additional mixed weaponry mounted externally, the two-seat A-1 was often used in support of ground actions.

The McDonnell Douglas A-4 Skyhawk was designed as a simple, low-cost light-weight attack and ground-support aircraft. It could reach a maximum speed of 645 mph. Its armament consisted of two standard 20-mm Mk-12 cannon in the wings and multiple variations of payload, including bombs, air-to-surface, and/or air-to-air rockets. "The Skyhawk," writes air historian Mark Clodfelter, "a diminutive, single-seat fighter that carried a 4-ton bomb load, flew more bombing missions [during Rolling Thunder] than any other naval aircraft in Vietnam."[40]

But the A-4, along with the air force's F-105 Thunderchief and the F-4 Phantom, the two other aircraft most often used for bombing runs, could not fly in poor weather. And an all-weather aircraft was a scarce commodity. "Only the A-6 Intruder flown by the Navy and Marines possessed all-weather capability," writes Clodfelter, "and only two A-6 squadrons (thirty-two aircraft) normally operated with CTF 77 [Carrier Task Force 77]."[41] Though few in number, the Intruders acquitted themselves well.

Conceived as a carrier-borne low-level attack bomber, the Grumman A-6 Intruder was specifically equipped to deliver nuclear or conventional weapons on targets totally obscured by weather or darkness. It could carry 18,000 pounds of bombs at speeds of 648 mph. On April 18, 1966, two A6-As from the carrier *Kitty Hawk* aptly demonstrated their deadly efficiency in a spectacular night

A group of A-4 Skyhawks are parked on the bow of the USS Enterprise.

raid on the Uongbi power plant near Haiphong. Scoring hits with all twenty-six of their 1,000-pound bombs, they knocked out one-third of North Vietnam's electric power production.

The Vought A-7 Corsair II, a light attack aircraft designed to replace the A-4 Skyhawk, flew at subsonic speed (691 mph), yielding a significant weight saving in terms of its engine and thus allowing it to carry a greater munitions load. The A-7 was armed with one forward-firing M61A1 20-mm Vulcan gun, and two under-fuselage and six under-wing stations enabled it to carry 15,000 pounds of external stores, that is, bombs, rockets, missiles, and the like.

The Corsair, along with the A-6 Intruder, was used extensively for strike missions during the Linebacker raids, with the F-4 Phantom usually providing fighter cover and flak suppression for the attack aircraft. On May 10, 1972, the first day of Linebacker I, navy pilots flew 294 sorties over North Vietnam from three carriers in the Gulf of Tonkin. Air force pilots contributed another 120 sorties on that day, which saw the heaviest one-day action of the war. American pilots shot down eleven MiGs while losing two F-4s in air-to-air engagements. Two additional F-4s succumbed to antiaircraft fire and ground-launched missiles. Navy pilots destroyed eight of the MiGs during the air fighting without loss.

Patrolling the Coast

While making vital contributions to the allied air and ground offensives, America's fleet was never challenged during its operations in the Vietnam War. Other than navy fliers, naval shipboard personnel in the Seventh Fleet who were killed during the war years were lost due to accidents rather than enemy action. The naval forces that did see action on the water were part of the patrols that plied Vietnam's coasts, rivers, and inland waterways. Their main task was to stop the movement of North Vietnamese supplies by water into the South. To accomplish this, the command was split into three task forces: TF 115, the Coastal Surveillance Force; TF 116, the River Patrol Force; and TF 117, the Riverine Assault Force.

The Coastal Surveillance Force (TF 115) was responsible for curtailing the seaborne infiltration of communist arms and supplies along the twelve-hundred-mile coastline of South Vietnam, from the 17th parallel to the Cambodian border. To facilitate search operations conducted by ships and aircraft of the U.S. Navy, the Coast Guard, and the South Vietnamese navy, the coastline was divided into nine patrol sectors. Commencing on March 11, 1965, the task force carried out Operation Market Time, which involved establishing three anti-infiltration barriers. First, and farthest from land, an air barrier was maintained with long-range patrol planes flying about 100 to 150 miles offshore. Next, and closer to shore, came an outer-surface barrier comprised of destroyer escorts, minesweepers, Coast Guard cutters, and similar craft. Nearest the coast was the inshore barrier, patrolled by Swift boats, 50-foot craft capa-

Intense Commitment

Dennis Barr, a former (maintenance) assistant plane captain on an A-7C Corsair attack aircraft aboard the U.S. carrier *America* during the Vietnam War, later reflected on all the men around him who helped to keep the Corsairs in the air. In "A Carrier at War," published in *Nam*, edited by Tim Page and John Pimlott, Barr writes:

> To keep a carrier air wing in combat you need more than mechanics, electronics technicians, fuel handlers and armament specialists. You also need to keep alive this floating city from which aviators come and go. This takes food, drink, a laundry, a dry cleaners, air conditioning, communications. The Hollywood stars of an attack carrier like the *America* are the brightly-clad deck crew-

men who risk their lives daily to attach a catapult bridle to a revved-up Intruder, or who maneuver Phantoms and Corsairs around the crowded deck in a blurred cacophony of noise and motion. But don't ever tell me that we could run the war without a 14-hour day from that crewcut Texan kid who works the ovens in the bakery, or the sweat and toil of that skinny black guy from Chicago who types up the ship's drill bulletin, the Plan of the Day. The cook, the tailor, and the typist may not get into the credits like a missile guidance technician or a catapult launch chief do, but it takes an intense commitment by every last manjack aboard the 1047-foot, 60,300-ton *America* to keep the carrier and its air wing in the war.

And how about the medics? Too often we've had to pull a pilot out of a bullet-ridden aircraft. Some guy suffering from a gut wound, a spraying from hot metal fragments, or grievous burns. The medical technicians and doctors who labor on our wounded deserve all the credit they can get.

A Vaught A-7 Corsair is prepared for takeoff. Many crewmen helped to keep the Corsairs in the air.

ble of 23 knots and armed with .50-caliber machine guns and an 81-mm mortar.

As testament to the effectiveness of Operation Market Time, General Westmoreland estimated that prior to 1965 the enemy "had received about 70 percent of his sup-

plies by sea; by the end of 1966, our best guess was that not more than 10 percent of his requirements arrived by that route."[42] The general may have based his estimate on sparse evidence, but even doubling his guess would leave a creditable effect.

The Brown Water Navy

Task Force 116 (TF 116)—better known as the River Patrol Force—was established in December 1965 to direct naval forces conducting Operation Game Warden, which was designed to deny the VC and NVA the use of some three thousand nautical miles of rivers, smaller streams, and canals. TF 116 comprised a number of river divisions, each with twenty large patrol boats, assorted smaller watercraft, and several aircraft. Patrol operations were headquartered in landing ships (LSTs and LSDs), which also served as floating base facilities.

Operation Game Warden commenced with a fleet of river patrol boats—Patrol Boat Riverine. The PBR, adapted from a civilian design, had a 31-foot-long and 10.5-inch wide fiberglass hull, with a draft (the part of the boat's hull under the water) of only 9–18 inches, making it ideal for operating in shallow waters. It was responsive, highly maneuverable, and could make up to twenty-five knots. Armed with twin .50-caliber machine guns forward, a .30-caliber machine gun aft, and a rapid-fire 40-mm grenade launcher, the PBR was crewed by four sailors.

In Vietnam, PBRs usually operated in pairs. These boats actively patrolled the rivers of South Vietnam, stopping any vessel that was suspected of carrying enemy contraband. Since the Viet Cong moved supplies in small skiffs (sampans) common to the fisherman and other civilians who lived along the river, the river patrols typically searched every craft they encountered. Like village searches conducted by the army, these boat searches irritated the South Vietnamese populace, who interpreted the continual stops as harassment. The Americans, however, conducted their searches with caution, believing that any vessel could be a threat. Apparently innocent civilian fishermen could have AK-47 assault rifles stashed just out of sight. The Viet Cong had also forced the Americans to be wary, blocking rivers with homemade mines, or booby trapping the cargo holds of their sampans with deadly devices ranging from high explosives to poisonous snakes.

Certainly, the American sailors did uncover enemy supplies during their searches, but the high number of sampans that plied the waters meant that some resources always got through. Yet like Operation Market Time, Operation Game Warden did have its effect, keeping the amount of contraband reaching the Viet Cong by river to a minimum. The Viet Cong, however, saw the river operations as more of an inconvenience than a real hindrance since supplies and weapons could still be moved overland.

The Riverine Assault Force

After the navy had policed the waterways, swamps, and rice paddies of South Vietnam for a little over two years in Operation Game Warden, the military command decided that what it really needed was a way to move troops in the Mekong Delta as quickly as it had achieved air mobility in other combat zones. After all, the delta was laced with over six thousand kilometers of natural and man-made waterways, perfect for conduct-

Quick, responsive, and highly maneuverable, Patrol Boats Riverine patrolled the rivers of South Vietnam.

ing waterborne operations. The decision resulted in the birth of the Mobile Riverine Force, a joint army-navy venture. General Westmoreland credits Capt. David F. Welch, a naval officer on his staff, with advancing the idea. "In much the same way that U.S. forces in, for example, the Seminole War and the Civil War had used waterways to facilitate military operations," Westmoreland writes, "why could we not create special units equipped to utilize the extensive waterways of the [Mekong] Delta to get at the Viet Cong."[43] The navy concurred. Activated on February 28, 1967, the Riverine Assault Force and SEAL teams formed the U.S. Navy's component of the Mobile Riverine Force, operating jointly with ground elements of the army's 9th Infantry Division, which were frequently joined by South Vietnamese Army and marine units.

The Mobile Riverine Force became operational in June 1967 and launched a series of operations in the Mekong Delta and the Rung Sat Special Zone (delta of the Saigon and Dong Nai Rivers) that lasted until April 1971. With the capability of moving its 5,000-man force 150 miles over water in twenty-four hours and engaging the enemy within a half hour of anchoring, the Mobile Riverine Force truly lived up to its name. Its prime objective was to clear the delta of Viet Cong activity, and open the one hard-surfaced road, Highway 4, that was the lifeline to the people and economy of the northern delta region. It was a daunting task, considering that eighty-five thousand Viet Cong operated in the area and had effectively shut down movement along Highway 4.

The Boats and Their Duties

The navy organized its Riverine Assault Force into four River Assault Squadrons of four hundred men each. A typical squadron consisted of two command control boats (CCBs), five monitors (the "battleships" of the force), twenty-six armored troop carriers (ATCs), and sixteen assault support and patrol boats (ASPBs). All but the latter were modified versions of the long, boxlike, vintage World War II mechanized landing craft used to bring troops ashore on such memorable events as the Normandy invasion.

In a given Mobile Riverine operation, these craft were supplemented by a variety of other craft, such as Swift boats, river patrol boats, mobile barges carrying a heavy-duty battalion of 105-mm howitzers, self-propelled barracks ships (APBs) to provide floating base facilities, and others. Of the diverse vessels in the riverine force, perhaps none stand out more than the monitors and the assault support and patrol boats.

The monitor was crewed by eleven men and provided the Mobile Riverine Force with a solid base of fire. It contained a 40-mm cannon and a .50-caliber machine gun in its forward turret, an 81-mm mortar and two M-60 machine guns mounted amidship, and one 20-mm cannon, two .50-caliber, and four M-60 machine guns carried aft. A few monitors were fitted with forward flamethrowers and sailors quickly dubbed them "Zippo" boats (after the popular cigarette lighter).

The fifty-foot assault support and patrol boat was the only boat designed and built from the keel up for riverine operations. Lighter and faster than the other boats, it displaced about thirty-five tons and could

Heavily armed, monitors provided deadly firepower to the Riverine Assault Force.

make fifteen knots. Crewed by six enlisted men, its one 20-mm gun, one 81-mm mortar, two .50-caliber machine guns, and two automatic grenade launchers added still more firepower to the Mobile Riverine Force's inventory. It led the way on riverine "ops," or operations, as described by Tim Page and John Pimlott, well-known chroniclers of the Vietnam War:

> The heavily armed ASPBs would take on the role of point as the column of boats plowed through the water, with minesweepers on both flanks. Next came the river assault commander in his CCB. A Monitor was usually the next craft in line, ready to unleash sustained firepower into the bushes on the river banks if any incoming was received. Then came a force of three ATCs carrying the battalion's first company [of troops to unload].[44]

Once ashore, the infantry could strike and take out enemy positions. The advantage to all this mechanization was mobility. Like their helicopter counterparts, the riverine forces could bring large numbers of men and firepower to strategically important regions in a short time—as long as such places were reachable by water, and most places in the Mekong Delta were.

The Riverine Assault Force, in conjunction with airborne operations in the delta, proved effective over its short tenure. Initial attacks on the Viet Cong surprised and confused the enemy, often yielding high casualties. But the Viet Cong learned to fight back, mining waterways and luring the assault boats into shore before attacking them with powerful recoilless-rifle fire. Overall, the American strategy was successful, evicting most Viet Cong units from the region by 1968. In that year, troop withdrawals reduced the number of infantry units in the 9th Division. By the following year, the navy handed over sixty-four river assault craft to the South Vietnamese Army during America's campaign to turn over the bulk of the fighting to the Saigon government. By that time, the Riverine Assault Force had reopened Highway 4 allowing goods from the northern delta region to reach ports for export, supporting South Vietnam's teetering economy.

Perhaps Unsung but Not Forgotten

With the face-to-face confrontations of the riverine forces, the airstrike capabilities of the carrier task force, and the mobile artillery support function of the destroyers, cruisers, and battleships of the Seventh Fleet, the U.S. Navy served many roles during the Vietnam conflict. Its contributions, however, are often overlooked in a war that came to be symbolized by the helicopter and the foot soldier. Yet no one who was there fighting inland would forget the valuable assistance of the *New Jersey's* 16-inch guns, or the suppressive bombings of navy planes, or the strategic maneuvers of the riverine forces that cut off enemy retreats. Its brave sailors share both in the victories and the final defeat of America's military presence in Vietnam.

Chapter 6

The Other War: The Battle for Hearts and Minds

On January 17, 1966, Gen. Wallace M. Greene, commandant of the U.S. Marine Corps, returned to Washington, D.C., from a thirteen-day tour of the war zone in Vietnam. His talks with military analysts and combat soldiers from the DMZ to the Mekong Delta had led him to a bleak conclusion: "You can kill every Viet Cong and North Vietnamese soldier," he asserted, "and still lose the war." The general now realized that winning the war would require more than the better tactics and overwhelming firepower that U.S. forces had so far employed against their enemy. "The real target[s] in Vietnam," General Greene said with conviction, "were not the VC and the North Vietnamese but the Vietnamese people."[45]

Greene was not the first U.S. leader to recognize that victory in Vietnam could not be achieved without "winning the hearts and minds" of the South Vietnamese people, nor would he be the last. Pacification, or "the other war," as it is fre-

quently called, began in 1956 and was implemented through various programs during most of the Vietnam War. As its name implies, the pacification strategy was employed to appease the South Vietnamese people who were defecting to the Viet Cong in droves. The reasons for the desertions were numerous but focused primarily on the abuses and unmet promises of the Saigon government as well as unprovoked harassment by American soldiers. Entire villages had been burned by American and ARVN troops hunting down Viet Cong, and innocent villagers were carted off in roundups of suspected enemy sympathizers. These acts—coupled with the fact that the battlefield was permanently rooted in South Vietnam—resulted in bitter resentment against the allied armies who came to be seen as occupiers instead of liberators. To counter this image, the American military decided it needed to adopt a new face, one that would paint the military as beneficent saviors, helping the South Vietnamese reinvigorate their damaged economy and ridding them of the misfortunes brought on by communist infiltrators.

Agrovilles and Strategic Hamlets

As early as 1959, U.S. advisors had seen the need for counterinsurgency measures. Before even considering the winning of hearts and minds, the Americans understood the necessity of protecting the populace from the Viet Cong. They encouraged the government of Ngo Dinh Diem to herd rural peasants into "agrovilles," fortified villages that were protected by military units in an effort to keep the Viet Cong from influencing civilians or seeking shelter in their unmonitored villages. But the peas-

ants resented being uprooted from their traditional homes to be moved into these sanctioned areas, even in the name of safety. They resented it even more when the government forced them to build their own agrovilles in return for vague promises of land, farm aid, and schools. Although the government ordered that eighty agrovilles be built, peasant resistance and Viet Cong aggression led to the program's abandonment in 1960.

Not to be denied, however, the Diem government launched a similar program

A group of soldiers erect a network of barbed wire defenses around a South Vietnamese village to secure it from Viet Cong infiltrators.

the following year. In essence, it was a modified version of the failed agroville experiment. Named the "strategic hamlet program," it called for villages to be cordoned off with barbed wire and other defenses and for the villagers to be armed and trained in basic defense. By such measures, the government hoped to transform hamlets into "antiguerrilla bastions" and thereby to oppose the Viet Cong with a network of armed camps organized into a "crisscrossed line of defense."[46]

With the government providing better aid than it had for the agrovilles, 3,235 strategic hamlets were created by the end of 1962, prompting South Vietnamese officials to claim that more than 66 percent of the population was safely harbored in fortified hamlets, supposedly protected by government troops. In truth, however, government troops often abandoned the hamlets at night, fearing they were not defensible. Even worse, fewer than 10 percent of the hamlets had any troop protection at all. The Viet Cong moved virtually unhindered about the countryside and obliterated individual strategic hamlets almost at will. Those they did not destroy, they infiltrated and sometimes led. In the latter case, the guerrillas were often grateful to receive the rifles and ammunition meant to be used in defense of the hamlet.

But all was not lost. One element of the strategic hamlet initiative—the *Chieu Hoi* (Open Arms) program, which offered clemency to Viet Cong defectors—yielded positive results throughout the war. A few Viet Cong defectors, generally known as "ralliers," even served as scouts for U.S. ground forces when they arrived. These former Viet Cong swore allegiance to South Vietnam and served on the front line with U.S. military units, often leading them to VC trails, caches, and strongholds.

The Need for Social Change

In retrospect, the agroville and strategic hamlet programs failed partly because of bureaucratic and operational mishandling, but mostly because of the Saigon government's failure to protect villagers from the Viet Cong. Not daunted by their early failures, the Saigon government and its American advisors turned away from offering mere physical protection, and decided to concentrate on strategies that would cater to the social and economic needs of the peasants in order to gain their confidence and allegiance. The war to win the hearts and minds of the South Vietnamese had begun.

Part of the new attempt to garner support from the rural peasants was still rooted in the defense of their villages. The American advisors and their ARVN diplomats tried to bolster patriotism among the villagers, giving them weapons and training them so they might have pride in keeping the scourge of the Viet Cong away from their families and neighbors. In some respects, this concept was valid; Viet Cong recruitment took sons and daughters away from village life just as service in the South Vietnamese Army would. But what the

Americans overestimated was the villagers' willingness to fight. Vietnam had been at war for decades, and the idea of going off to war was certainly not met with enthusiasm, especially when rice fields needed to be planted and harvested. Besides, the South Vietnamese had been oppressed by the corrupt Diem government, which taxed the peasants and failed to deliver any social services. Furthermore, the peasants felt much more kinship with the North Vietnamese than the Americans, who were

Combined Action Platoons

One of the most effective innovations in the pacification campaign conducted in South Vietnam was the Combined Action Platoon, introduced by the U.S. Marine Corps in 1965. In *A Fellowship of Valor,* former marine combat commander Joseph H. Alexander explains the concept:

> Beginning quietly in 1965, and spreading rapidly throughout Eye [I] Corps in subsequent years, was a Marine Corps innovation known as the "Combined Action Platoon." The CAP concept was simple. A hand-picked, carefully trained (language, customs, weaponry) Marine rifle squad, with a Navy medical corpsman attached, would be assigned to a village to be integrated with several dozen Popular Forces troops [peasants assigned to defend a village under the pacification program], the much-maligned, barely trained local militia. The Marines would move into the village to stay (sleep, eat, fight), patiently teaching military skills and virtues to the PFs, in exchange for their intelligence about local VC operations. Cultural misunderstandings abounded, but gradually—some said, *miraculously*—the PFs and other villagers accepted the Marine presence, gained confidence, and began producing villages and hamlets that were secure day *and night.* In nocturnal firefights against the VC, some PFs "skied" [fled] at first, but most stayed to fight shoulder-to-shoulder with the Leathernecks. In the words of General Brute Krulak: "The Vietnamese knew who the guerrillas were and where they hid; the Marines knew how to kill them." Before long the number of CAPs grew to the size of a full regiment, which made the top brass in Saigon uncomfortable. They thought the Marines should stop frittering away their resources in civic action projects and get on with the grandiose "search and destroy" missions which were sure to bring victory. . . .

> Despite its unpopularity at the highest levels, the CAP Program was the major and most successful Marine Corps contribution to the Vietnam War.

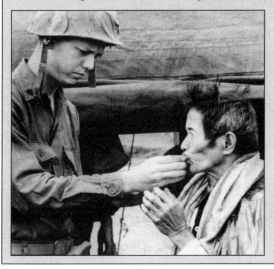

A corpsman administers medicine to a Vietnamese villager while part of a Combined Action Platoon.

yet another occupying foreign army, as the French had been in previous decades.

A Series of Imperfect Programs

What the Americans had to prove was that social, political, and economic change could come about under the Saigon government. To gain the confidence of the people, American officials prompted Saigon to institute welfare programs that distributed emergency food rations and medical supplies to areas in need. These programs also sponsored a rebuilding of the nation's infrastructure, repairing bridges and assisting local economies. For the most part these programs helped specific villages, but Saigon officials—who were still concerned about the shooting war—were slow to expand the programs to broad areas.

Reaching this stage of the pacification process, however, meant that the threat of the Viet Cong had been removed from a region. And in 1964, the U.S. introduced a revised pacification plan named *Chien Thang* (Will to Victory) that was intended to slowly increase the boundaries of pacified areas. Called the "ink-blot" or "oil-on-water" approach, the idea was to institute the rebuilding efforts in a core group of villages while continually spreading out and reclaiming more villages from the

The Revolutionary Development (RD) program attempted to strengthen the security of villages while providing economic and political advice.

Viet Cong. Once emptied of Viet Cong, these villages would then benefit from economic and social programs. The success of the ink-blot strategy relied on the work of the U.S. and ARVN troops clearing villages of Viet Cong, a difficult task that always faltered considering the number of soldiers necessary to keep expanding the ring of secured villages. Because most military leaders were concerned with fighting large Viet Cong units, not hunting down stray members or sympathizers in the villages, few "ink-blots" spread very far.

Next in line in the string of pacification strategies came the national Revolutionary Development (RD) program—called Rural Construction by Saigon, a government-directed program implemented by special civilian units known as People's Action Teams. Introduced in 1965, the RD plan was instituted by the South Vietnamese government to help strengthen local civilian security of villages while also offering political and economic advice. The program was backed by U.S. funds and supplies, and it enjoyed some success and lasted until cuts in U.S. aid forced its disbanding in 1971. The Revolutionary Development program was the first program to establish a direct link between the Saigon government and the people. But the RD plan still failed to win the full support of the military and led indirectly to the creation of the Civil Operations and Revolutionary Development Support (CORDS) program, which lent new impetus to pacification.

CORDS

Created in 1967 by a Johnson administration burdened with criticisms over the shooting war and eager to improve U.S. prosecution of "the other war," CORDS was headed by strong-willed Robert W. Komer. Komer, brought to the White House in March 1966 as a special presidential advisor, was charged with directing and coordinating Washington-level support for pacification. Nicknamed "the blowtorch," Komer brought both ideas and action to his new assignment. While maintaining that pacification programs in Vietnam should fall under overall military authority, Komer pushed for civilian control of all pacification resources. Since the American military was more concerned with fighting the North Vietnamese, and the South Vietnamese military was often unconcerned with the peasants, Komer believed civilian authority would help get pacification efforts moving.

In May 1967, Johnson sent Komer to Vietnam to put his theories into operation. Appointed to the rank of ambassador and named deputy to the U.S. military commander in Vietnam, Komer organized CORDS, which combined under a single command personnel and resources from the military services, the State Department, and various aid agencies that had been functioning rather haphazardly in previous years. Its aim was "establishing or re-establishing local government responsive to and involving the people." To accomplish this, the program was to promote the following: "the provision of sustained, credible territory security, the

*Members of CORDS attempted to aid
Vietnamese peasants in any way possible.*

The combined agencies of CORDS reached out across South Vietnam, deploying unified civil-military teams in all of the nation's forty-four provinces and 250 districts. It placed American and South Vietnamese civilian advisory teams into hundreds of villages, working to aid the peasants in any way possible, from inoculating children against disease to helping irrigate rice fields. Evaluating CORDS's effectiveness, Harry G. Summers Jr. said of the program, "A remarkable improvement over previous attempts at pacification, this approach eventually led to the virtual elimination of the Viet Cong threat to South Vietnam."[48]

The Phoenix Program

destruction of the enemy's underground government, the assertion or reassertion of political control and involvement of the people in government, and the initiation of economic and social activity capable of self-sustenance and expansion."[47] These were effectively the same aims that previous programs had attempted, but with Komer in charge, the poor cooperation between military, political, and civilian authorities that had plagued past efforts, was overcome.

That "elimination"—though helped by the peaceful efforts of aid workers—also resulted from the darker aspects of the CORDS program. Improvements in creature comforts and social reform pacified many peasants who had not seen such cooperation from the Saigon government before, but the Viet Cong insurgents still tempted some with the promise of a better life through worker-controlled government and the eviction of occupying armies. These instigators had to be dealt with even under the new program of pacification. To neutralize the Viet Cong sympathizers, CORDS adopted the highly controversial Phoenix program.

The Phoenix program was laid out by Robert Komer in 1967 and put into effect by South Vietnamese president Nguyen Van Thieu (the third military man to run the Saigon government after Diem's assassination) in July 1968. Called *Phung Hoang* by the South Vietnamese, the operation was primarily to be carried out by the South Vietnamese government. "Phoenix was meant to be a South Vietnamese project with U.S. advisors," notes Dale Andradé of the U.S. Army Center of Military History. "Roughly, Phung Hoang was the actual intelligence and operations side and Phoenix was the U.S. advisory effort that paralleled Phung Hoang."[49] The goal of the Phoenix program was to use army intelligence and CIA files to identify some seventy thousand

Pointed Questions

At one point during the Phoenix pacification program, the Saigon government claimed "control" over 90 percent of South Vietnam's villages. But historian John Prados poses some pointed questions in *The Hidden History of the Vietnam War:*

> The question is, how much *loyalty* did control buy? How many hearts and minds were won?

> These discussions of pacification also assume that anything gained came as a direct result of American or South Vietnamese initiatives, whether from Phoenix or other, less sinister programs. This ignores the degree to which the Viet Cong themselves lost the hearts and minds of villagers through their tax collections, involuntary recruitment of men and women, assassinations, and other exactments. The account Le Ly Hayslip has written of growing up in a South Vietnamese village which at first was united against the foreign (American) invader and local collaborators, then at length soured on the dogmatic Viet Cong, is telling in this regard. But loss of loyalty to the VC was not the same as giving one's heart to Saigon, especially since Saigon saw the war situation as enabling it to discontinue the programs that benefited villagers.

Despite propaganda from both sides in the war, villagers could see that neither side was especially amenable to their needs. Villagers could also see that the old war of the Viet Cong guerrillas was increasingly being supplanted by the new war of regular forces in conventional combat. Under the circumstances, the incentives for Vietnamese villagers were increasingly to take no side in the war. [William E.] Colby [who coordinated the Phoenix program] could drive at night because the villagers preferred to stay out of the fighting, not because Saigon had pacified South Vietnam.

Winning the "hearts and minds" of Vietnamese villagers proved to be a task easier said than done.

members of the Viet Cong hierarchy—the political leaders, recruiters and indoctrinators, and other high-level Communist Party members responsible for terrorist activities and untold thousands of assassinations within South Vietnam. The South Vietnamese National Police would then round up the dissidents and try them for treason.

The program ran with incredible effectiveness, though some critics referred to it as a terror campaign. In their zeal to incarcerate suspected Viet Cong, the South Vietnamese police and even the American advisory staff committed numerous violations of victims' civil rights. Reports of torture and assassination of prisoners were not uncommon. The program's American director, William E. Colby, adamantly denied these accusations. "To call it a program of murder is nonsense," he scoffed. "[The Viet Cong] were of more value to us alive than dead, and therefore the object was to try to get them alive."[50] Historians, however, disagree, though they tend to stipulate that most slayings came at the hands of the South Vietnamese police and not of American advisors.

Overall, the Phoenix program did not accomplish as much as it set out to do, but it had an undeniable effect on the Viet Cong. In 1981, Nguyen Co Thach, foreign minister of Vietnam after 1975, told Pulitzer Prize–winning journalist Stanley Karnow that the Phoenix effort "wiped out many of our bases,"[51] forcing many Viet Cong troops to seek sanctuary in Cambodia instead of in the villages of South Vietnam. The Phoenix program was also the last effort Americans would make in the "war" of pacification.

Peace with Honor or Utter Failure?

On June 8, 1969, President Richard Nixon met with South Vietnamese president Nguyen Van Thieu at Midway Island for six hours to discuss the Paris peace talks, the current battlefront situation, and South Vietnam's assumption of a larger role in the fighting. Over the objections of both Thieu and American commanders, Nixon announced his decision to pursue a policy of "Vietnamization," or turning the war effort over to the South Vietnamese while withdrawing American troops from the conflict.

Facing pressures from the American public, who had now witnessed America's longest war with no end in sight, Nixon opted to pursue what he called "peace with honor." He intended to end America's military involvement and compensate by delivering huge amounts of war matériel to the South Vietnamese to carry on the fight. It was an executive decision to cut the nation's losses and run, knowing full well that the ARVN forces could not hope to adequately defend their country against the Viet Cong and NVA onslaught. The war dragged on for four more years as the exchange of command took place and U.S. troops were slowly pulled off the firing line and brought home. The NVA waited out the process of American troop withdrawal, until finally U.S. military commitment ended in 1973. For two

Americans are evacuated from the roof of the U.S. Embassy in Saigon as South Vietnam falls to communist forces.

years, the United States tried to bolster South Vietnam's fighting strength with its promised aid, but Congress reduced the aid packages before they were sent. The NVA and Viet Cong staged a spring offensive in 1975 after pushing the demoralized ARVN troops back in nearly every battle in those intervening years. On April 30, 1975, while victorious Viet Cong and North Vietnamese soldiers marched into the streets of Saigon, the last Americans in Vietnam were being airlifted from the roof of the American embassy to waiting ships at sea.

America had failed to win the war in Vietnam despite the fact that it could claim military victory in every major campaign. But besides failing to defeat the enemy, the Americans also failed in their efforts to win the hearts and minds of the South Vietnamese people. Their pacification programs did deliver aid to the populace, but the continual warfare ensured that the Americans would not be embraced by the people. South Vietnam had remained a battlefield

for so many years that the mere presence of the Americans soldiers simply signified that this would not change. In addition, the U.S. government had similarly failed to win the hearts and minds of its own citizens, who were demonstrating in the streets of American cities that the people did not stand unified behind continued involvement in Vietnam. This division sent a clear message to the South Vietnamese that America's commitment was uncertain and liable to leave supporters of the Saigon government high and dry when eventual withdrawal occurred. The vast number of peasants in South Vietnam had survived decades of warfare, and when it came down to proving allegiance, they—like so many other defenseless people caught up in war—did only what their hearts and minds told them: Continue to survive in any way possible.

★ Notes ★

Introduction: The Vietnam Experience

1. Quoted in Marilyn B. Young, *The Vietnam Wars, 1945–1990*. New York: Harper Collins, 1991, p. 80.
2. Quoted in Young, *The Vietnam Wars*, pp. 80–81.
3. Quoted in Young, *The Vietnam Wars*, p. 81.

Chapter 1: First In: The Special Forces

4. Quoted in Michael Lee Lanning and Dan Cragg, *Inside the VC and the NVA: The Real Story of North Vietnam's Armed Forces*. New York: Fawcett Columbine, 1992, p. 81.
5. Hans Halberstadt, *War Stories of the Green Berets: The Viet Nam Experience*. Osceola, Wl: Motorbooks International, 1994, p. 80.
6. James F. Dunnigan and Albert A. Nofi, *Dirty Little Secrets of the Vietnam War*. New York: St. Martin's, 1999, p. 197.
7. Shelby L. Stanton, *Green Berets at War: U.S. Army Special Forces in Southeast Asia, 1956–1975*. New York: Ballantine, 1999, p. 5.
8. Rod Paschall, "Fighting with the Hill Tribesmen," in Tim Page and John Pimlott, cons. eds., *Nam The Vietnam Experience 1965–1975*. New York: Mallard, 1990, p. 205.
9. Rod Macon, "Special Operations Group," in Page and Pimlott, *Nam*, p. 455.
10. Paschall, "Fighting with the Hill Tribesmen," p. 206.
11. Quoted in John L. Plaster, *SOG: The Secret Wars of America's Commandos in Vietnam*. New York: Penguin Putnam, 1998, p. 357.
12. Stanton, *Green Berets at War*, p. 305.
13. Quoted in Plaster, *SOG*, p. 357.

Chapter 2: Overcoming the Jungle: The Ground War

14. Quoted in Page and Pimlott, "Into the Nam," in *Nam*, p. 7.
15. Joseph H. Alexander, with Don Horan and Norman C. Stahl, *A Fellowship of Valor: The Battle History of the United States Marines*. New York: Harper-Collins, 1997, p. 320.
16. Quoted in Bernard C. Nalty, ed., *The Vietnam War: The History of America's Conflict in Southeast Asia*. Classic Conflicts series. London: Salamander, 1998, p. 113.
17. Alexander, *A Fellowship of Valor*, p. 325.
18. Quoted in Edward Doyle, Samuel Lipsman, and the Editors of Boston

Publishing, *America Takes Over, 1965–67.* The Vietnam Experience series. Boston: Boston Publishing, 1982. p. 116.

19. Quoted in Doyle and Lipsman, *America Takes Over,* p. 116.

Chapter 3: Mobility and Firepower: U.S. Weapons

20. David Miller, "Weapons and Warfare Techniques Used in Vietnam," in Ray Bonds, ed., *The Vietnam War: Illustrated History of the Conflict in Southeast Asia.* New York: Crown, 1983, p. 28.

21. David H. Hackworth and Julie Sherman, *About Face: The Odyssey of an American Warrior.* New York: Simon & Schuster, 1989, pp. 488–89.

22. John Pimlott, *Vietnam: The Decisive Battles.* New York: Macmillan, 1990, p. 78.

23. Quoted in James R. Wilson, *Landing Zones: Combat Vets from America's Proud, Fighting South Remember Vietnam.* New York: Pocket, 1993, pp. 23–24.

24. H. Norman Schwarzkopf, with Peter Petre, *It Doesn't Take a Hero: The Autobiography.* New York: Bantam, 1992, p. 122.

25. Quoted in Page and Pimlott, "Gunslingers," in *Nam,* p. 435.

26. B. G. Burkett and Glenna Whitley, *Stolen Valor: How the Vietnam Generation Was Robbed of Its Heroes and Its History.* Dallas: Verity Press, 1998, p. 622, note 9.

27. Burkett and Whitley, *Stolen Valor,* pp. 24–25.

Chapter 4: Rolling Thunder: The Air War

28. Quoted in Young, *The Vietnam Wars,* p. 130.

29. Quoted in Young, *The Vietnam Wars,* p. 131.

30. Quoted in Doyle and Lipsman, *America Takes Over,* p. 35.

31. Walter J. Boyne, *Beyond the Wild Blue: A History of the United States Air Force 1947–1997.* New York: St. Martin's, 1997, p. 164.

32. Marshall L. Michel III, *Clashes: Air Combat over North Vietnam, 1965–1972.* Annapolis, MD: Naval Institute Press, 1997, p. 11.

33. Quoted in Doyle and Lipsman, *America Takes Over,* p. 177.

34. Quoted in Boyne, *Beyond the Wild Blue,* p. 161.

35. Boyne, *Beyond the Wild Blue,* pp. 161–62.

Chapter 5: Inland and Offshore: Naval Engagements

36. Quoted in Nalty, *The Vietnam War,* pp. 81–82.

37. Quoted in R. L. Schreadley, *From the Rivers to the Sea: The United States Navy in Vietnam.* Annapolis, MD: Naval Institute Press, 1992, p. 67.

38. Quoted in Nalty, *The Vietnam War,* p. 82.

39. Neil Sheehan, *A Bright Shining Lie: John Paul Vann and America in Vietnam.* New York: Vintage, 1989, p. 584.

40. Quoted in Mark Clodfelter, *The Limits of Airpower: The American Bombing of North Vietnam.* New York: Free Press, 1989, p. 133.

41. Clodfelter, *The Limits of Airpower*, p. 133.

42. Quoted in Terrence Maitland, Peter McInerney, and the Editors of Boston Publishing Company, *A Contagion of War*. The Vietnam Experience Series. Boston: Boston Publishing, 1983, p. 130.

43. Quoted in Schreadley, *From the Rivers to the Sea*, pp. 103–104.

44. Page and Pimlott, "The Brown Water Navy," in *Nam*, p. 259.

Chapter 6: The Other War: The Battle for Hearts and Minds

45. Quoted in Maitland and McInerney, *A Contagion of War*, p. 56.

46. Quoted in Dale Andradé, "Pacification," in Stanley I. Kutler, ed. *Encyclopedia of the Vietnam War*. New York: MacMillan, 1996, p. 418.

47. Quoted in Ronald H, Spector, *After Tet: The Bloodiest Year in Vietnam*. New York: Free Press, 1993, p. 279.

48. Harry G. Summers Jr., *Vietnam War Almanac*. New York: Facts On File, 1985, p. 133.

49. Andradé, "Pacification," p. 422.

50. Quoted in Samuel Lipsman, Edward Doyle, and the Editors of Boston Publishing Company, *Fighting for Time*. The Vietnam Experience Series. Boston: Boston Publishing, 1983, p. 80.

51. Quoted in Stanley Karnow, *Vietnam: A History*. New York: Viking, 1991, p. 617.

⭐ For Further Reading ⭐

Mark Baker, *Nam: The Vietnam War in the Words of the Men and Women Who Fought There*. New York: Berkley, 1983. An oral history of the war, in the voices of those who put their lives on the line in Vietnam.

T. L. Bosiljevac, *SEALs: UDT/SEAL Operations in Vietnam*. New York: Ballantine, 1991. Tales of a few brave men who help to build the reputation of the SEALs for special warfare.

R. D. Camp, with Eric Hammel, *Lima-6*. New York: Pocket, 1989. A former marine officer stands witness to the incredible courage of his fellow combat marines in Vietnam.

Philip Caputo, *A Rumor of War*. New York: Holt, Rinehart and Winston, 1977. A deeply personal memoir of the savagery and communion experienced by men at war.

Tom Carhart, *Battlefront Vietnam*. New York: Warner Books, 1991. Authoritatively reveals how American tactics and firepower won battle after battle but lost the war.

J. D. Coleman, *Choppers*. New York: St. Martin's, 1989. Recreates the battle for Pleiku, the birthplace and bloody testing ground of the newly formed air-assault forces of the U.S. Army's 1st Cavalry Division.

Clark Dougan, Stephen Weiss, and the Editors of Boston Publishing Company, *Nineteen Six-Eight*. The Vietnam Experience series. Boston: Boston Publishing, 1983. This volume concentrates on the year when American fortunes in Vietnam began a downward spiral.

Peter Goldman and Tony Fuller, with Richard Manning, et al., *Charlie Company: What Vietnam Did to Us*. New York: William Morrow, 1983. A collective memoir of the members of an American rifle company at war in Vietnam and afterward.

Donald M. Goldstein, Katherine V. Dillon, and J. Michael Wenger, *The Vietnam War: The Story and the Photographs*. Herndon, VA: Brassey's, 1999. The story and images of the war that shaped an entire generation.

Robert Leckie, *The Wars of America*. vol. 2. New York: HarperPerennial, 1993. A comprehensive recounting of America's conflicts from World War I to the Persian Gulf War, including a useful narrative of the Vietnam War.

Alex Lee, *Force Recon Command: 3rd Force Recon Company in Vietnam, 1969–1970*. New York: Ballantine, 1996. A gripping account of marines going nose-to-nose with the North Vietnamese Army.

The Library of America, *Reporting Vietnam*, 2 vols. Part One: *American Journalism, 1959–1969.* Part Two: *American Journalism, 1969–1975.* New York: Literary Classics of the United States, 1998. An anthology of superb reportage of the Vietnam War, drawn from original newspaper and magazine reports and contemporary books.

Maurice Matloff, ed., *American Military History. Vol. 2: 1902–1996.* Conshohocken, PA: Combined Books, 1996. The military history of America since 1902, viewed from both outward- and inward-looking perspectives.

Charles D. Melson, *The War That Would Not End: U.S. Marines in Vietnam, 1971–1973.* Central Point, OR: Hellgate, 1998. Marines battle for the northern provinces in the final phase of the ground war in Vietnam.

Edward F. Murphy, *Semper Fi Vietnam: From Da Nang to the DMZ, Marine Corps Campaigns, 1965–1975.* Novato, CA: Presidio, 1997. From major battles to minor skirmishes, this is the story of the U.S. Marines in action in Vietnam.

Stewart O'Nan, ed., *The Vietnam Reader.* New York: Doubleday, 1998. A broad collection of notable American fiction and nonfiction on the Vietnam War.

John Prados and Ray W. Stubbe, *Valley of Decision: The Siege of Khe Sanh.* New York: Dell, 1991. The unsurpassed, definitive account of seventy-seven days at Khe Sanh.

Samuel Zaffiri, *Hamburger Hill: May 11–20, 1969.* Novato, CA: Presidio, 1988. An intensely personal look at one of the Vietnam War's most misunderstood battles.

★ Works Consulted ★

Joseph H. Alexander, with Don Horan and Norman C. Stahl, *A Fellowship of Valor: The Battle History of the United States Marines*. New York: HarperCollins, 1997. A definitive single-volume history of the marines.

Robert B. Asprey, *War in the Shadows: The Guerrilla in History*, vol. 2. Garden City, NY: Doubleday, 1975. A finely crafted history of guerrilla warfare; includes valuable information about the Viet Cong and the Vietnam War.

Michael Bilton and Kevin Sim, *Four Hours in My Lai*. New York: Viking, 1992. The most complete account of the most notorious American war crime in history.

Ray Bonds, ed., *The Vietnam War: The Illustrated History of the Conflict in Southeast Asia*. New York: Crown, 1983. An action-filled, well-written history containing a battle-by-battle analysis of more than thirty years of open warfare in Southeast Asia.

Walter J. Boyne, *Beyond the Wild Blue: A History of the United States Air Force 1947–1997*. New York: St. Martin's, 1997. An intriguing account of fifty turbulent years of air force history.

B. G. Burkett and Glenna Whitley, *Stolen Valor: How the Vietnam Generation Was Robbed of Its Heroes and Its History*. Dallas, TX: Verity Press, 1998. An important work exposing the lies and myths of the Vietnam War and its ongoing aftermath.

Chuck Carlock, *Firebirds*. New York: Bantam Books, 1997. A harrowing firsthand account of helicopter combat in Vietnam.

Larry Chambers, *Death in the A Shau Valley: L Company LRRPs in Vietnam, 1969–70*. New York: Ballantine, 1998. A firsthand look at the men who scouted the enemy in the North Vietnamese Army's most forbidden valley.

John Whiteclay Chambers II, ed. in chief, *The Oxford Companion to American Military History*. New York: Oxford University Press, 1999. A bountiful treasury of information on American military history.

Mark Clodfelter, *The Limits of Airpower: The American Bombing of North Vietnam*. New York: Free Press, 1989. A penetrating critique of air power and its limitations as exemplified by the three major American bombing campaigns in Vietnam.

Phillip B. Davidson, *Vietnam at War: The History 1946–1975*. New York: Oxford University Press, 1988. General Westmoreland's former intelligence chief traces the course of the Vietnam War, from the initial French skirmishes in 1946 to the fall of Saigon in 1975.

Ron Dick, *American Eagles: A History of the United States Air Force*. Charlottesville, VA:

Howell, 1997. A bold tale told with insightful text, illustrated with lavish photographs by Dan Patterson.

Kevin Dockery and Bill Fawcett, eds., *The Teams: An Oral History of the U.S. Navy SEALs*. New York: William Morrow, 1998. Real-life exploits of the no-holds-barred, elite fighting teams of the U.S. Navy.

Frederick Downs, *The Killing Zone: My Life in the Vietnam War*. New York: Berkley, 1983. The story of Platoon Delta One-Six by its platoon leader.

Edward Doyle, Samuel Lipsman, and the Editors of Boston Publishing Company, *America Takes Over, 1965–67*. The Vietnam Experience series. Boston: Boston Publishing, 1982. America goes to war in Vietnam: the first three years of open warfare.

James F. Dunnigan and Albert A. Nofi, *Dirty Little Secrets of the Vietnam War*. New York: St. Martin's, 1999. A compendium of little-known facts about the Vietnam War.

Bernard B. Fall, *Hell in a Very Small Place: The Siege of Dien Bien Phu*. Philadelphia: J. B. Lippincott, 1967. Captures like no other book or reportage the essence of the fifty-six-day siege that kicked the French out of Vietnam.

———, *Street Without Joy: The Bloody Road to Dien Bien Phu*. Mechanicsburg, PA: Stackpole, 1994. A powerful history of the eight-year war that brought an end to French colonial rule in Indochina.

Bill Fawcett, ed., *Hunters & Shooters: An Oral History of the U.S. Navy SEALs in Vietnam*. New York: Avon, 1995. Fifteen former SEALs share their vivid remembrances of combat action during the Vietnam War.

Frances FitzGerald, *Fire in the Lake: The Vietnamese and the Americans in Vietnam*. Boston: Little, Brown, 1972. One of the first—and still one of the best—accounts of America's involvement in Vietnam.

Norman Franks, *Aircraft Versus Aircraft: The Illustrated Story of Fighter Pilot Combat from 1914 to the Present Day*. London: Grub Street, 1998. A fascinating story of pilots and their planes.

David H. Hackworth and Julie Sherman, *About Face: The Odyssey of an American Warrior*. New York: Simon & Schuster, 1989. Biography of a true American hero whose battlefield achievements in Korea and Vietnam have made him a legendary character in his own time.

Hans Halberstadt, *War Stories of the Green Berets: The Viet Nam Experience*. Osceola, WI: Motorbooks International, 1994. A collection of accounts of the U.S. Army Special Forces in action in Vietnam.

Eric Hammel, *The Siege of Khe Sanh: An Oral History*. New York: Warner Books, 1990. First-person accounts of the men who fought and survived the terrifying siege of Khe Sanh.

William M. Hammond, *Reporting Vietnam: Media and Military at War*. Lawrence: University Press of Kansas, 1998. A strong challenge to the many assertions by military leaders that the news media lost the Vietnam War by swaying public opinion against it.

Charles Henderson, *Marine Sniper: 93 Confirmed Kills.* Briarcliff Manor, NY: Stein and Day, 1986. Gripping biography of Carlos Hathcock, the top marine sniper in the Vietnam War.

Stanley Karnow, *Vietnam: A History.* New York: Viking, 1991. A classic account of America's war in Vietnam, rich in detail, with a sure grasp of the issues surrounding American involvement.

Jeffrey Kimball, *Nixon's Vietnam War.* Lawrence: University Press of Kansas, 1998. After years of secret negotiations, threats, and diplomacy, the president had to settle for a peace that fell far short of his original aims.

Charles H. Krohn, *The Lost Battalion: Controversy and Casualties in the Battle of Hue.* Westport, CT: Praeger, 1993. The story of an obscure battle fought outside Hue by the 2nd Battalion of the 1st Air Cavalry Division's 12th Cavalry regiment during Tet 1968.

Ed Kugler, *Dead Center: A Marine Sniper's Two-Year Odyssey in the Vietnam War.* New York: Ballantine, 1999. Brimming with firsthand accounts of sniper action in the Vietnam War.

Stanley I. Kutler, ed., *Encyclopedia of the Vietnam War.* New York: MacMillan, 1996. The definitive reference on America's longest war.

Michael Lee Lanning and Dan Cragg, *Inside the VC and the NVA: The Real Story of North Vietnam's Armed Forces.* New York: Fawcett Columbine, 1992. A rare book about the war as seen from the enemy's perspective.

Timothy M. Laur and Steven L. Llanso, The Army Times, Navy Times, Air Force Times *Encyclopedia of Modern U.S. Military Weapons.* Edited by Walter J. Boyne. New York: Berkley, 1998. An exhaustively researched volume of the weapons, vehicles, equipment, and systems of the U.S. armed forces.

Jack Leninger, *Time Heals No Wounds.* New York: Ballantine, 1993. The agony of the ground soldier's war in Vietnam told by a soldier who survived it.

Robert Jay Lifton, *Home from the War: Vietnam Veterans: Neither Victims nor Executioners.* New York: Simon & Schuster, 1973. A benchmark book on therapy for the survivors of counterinsurgency warfare in Vietnam.

Samuel Lipsman, Edward Doyle, and the Editors of Boston Publishing Company, *Fighting for Time.* The Vietnam Experience series. Boston: Boston Publishing, 1983. The search for peace, the politics of disengagement, and the continuing war in Vietnam during 1969–1970.

Terrence Maitland, Peter McInerney, and the Editors of Boston Publishing Company, *A Contagion of War.* The Vietnam Experience series. Boston: Boston Publishing, 1983. A companion volume to *America Takes Over,* featuring a sampling of the countless battles and ongoing pacification activities during 1965–1967.

Tom Mangold and John Penycate, *The Tunnels of Cu Chi.* New York: Berkley, 1986. A nerve-twisting account of the little-known underground war fought between American "tunnel rats" and the Viet Cong.

Charles Messenger, *The Century of Warfare: Worldwide Conflict from 1900 to the Present Day*. New York: HarperCollins, 1995. A treatise on war that favors no side and endeavors only to increase the reader's understanding of war in all its forms.

Marshall L. Michel III, *Clashes: Air Combat over North Vietnam, 1965–1972*. Annapolis, MD: Naval Institute Press, 1997. A balanced, extensive, and descriptive analysis of fighter combat over North Vietnam.

David Miller, *Special Forces: The Men, the Weapons, and the Operations*. London: Salamander, 1999. Possibly the most comprehensive reference work on the subject ever published.

Harold G. Moore and Joseph L. Galloway, *We Were Soldiers Once . . . and Young: Ia Drang: The Battle That Changed the War in Vietnam*. New York: Random House, 1992. Considered by many to be the classic book about battle in Vietnam, where heroism and horror coexisted.

Bernard C. Nalty, ed., *The Vietnam War: The History of America's Conflict in Southeast Asia*. Classic Conflicts series. London: Salamander, 1998. A detailed account of every aspect of the Vietnam War.

Keith William Nolan, *Battle for Hue: Tet, 1968*. Novato, CA: Presidio, 1983. The definitive account of the battle for Hue; compelling, accurate, and sensitive to both the comedy and tragedy of war.

———, *Death Valley: The Summer Offensive, I Corps, August 1969*. Novato, CA: Presidio, 1999. The story of combined U.S. Army and Marine forces in action against North Vietnamese Army forces southwest of Da Nang.

———, *The Magnificent Bastards: The Joint Army-Marine Defense of Dong Ha, 1968*. A hair-raising account of the nightmarish struggle for a strategic hamlet near a marine combat base.

Tim Page and John Pimlott, con. eds., *Nam: The Vietnam Experience 1965–1975*. New York: Mallard, 1990. A master volume on the Vietnam era, containing specially commissioned chapters written by men who were there; unmatched in its scope.

John Pimlott, *Vietnam: The Decisive Battles*. New York: Macmillan, 1990. Vivid accounts of seventeen major battles; well written and enhanced by photographs, illustrations, and computer graphics.

John L. Plaster, *SOG: The Secret Wars of America's Commandos in Vietnam*. New York: Penguin Putnam, 1998. Volunteers of the ultrasecret elite force code-named Studies and Observation Group did it all—sabotage, espionage, hand-to-hand combat, and more.

Ronald E. Powaski, *The Cold War: The United States and the Soviet Union, 1917–1991*. New York: Oxford University Press, 1998. Covers the major issues of the protracted struggle in a highly readable format.

John Prados, *The Hidden History of the Vietnam War*. Chicago: Ivan R. Dee, 1995. The author focuses on key strategies, issues, battle actions, and personalities to debunk popular myths and misconceptions about the Vietnam War.

John Quick, *Dictionary of Weapons & Military Terms*. New York: McGraw-Hill, 1973. A comprehensive record of the significant weapons developed over the centuries by armies all over the world.

R. L. Schreadley, *From the Rivers to the Sea: The United States Navy in Vietnam*. Annapolis, MD: Naval Institute Press, 1992. A concise yet thorough reference for anyone wanting to know about U.S. naval operations in Vietnam.

H. Norman Schwarzkopf, with Peter Petre, *It Doesn't Take a Hero: The Autobiography*. New York: Bantam, 1992. The triumphant story of a soldier true to his credo: duty, honor, and country.

Jonathan Shay, *Achilles in Vietnam: Combat Trauma and the Undoing of Character*. New York: Simon & Schuster, 1994. An original, scholarly work that views the trauma of combat in Vietnam through the comparative prism of Homer's *Iliad*.

Neil Sheehan, *A Bright Shining Lie: John Paul Vann and America in Vietnam*. New York: Vintage, 1989. A powerful biographical work that illuminates the fatal contradictions that led to American defeat in Vietnam.

Edwin H. Simmons, *The Illustrated History of the Marines: The Vietnam War*. New York: Bantam Books, 1987. A brief, illustrated history by a former commander of the 9th Marines.

Howard R. Simpson, *Dien Bien Phu: The Epic Battle America Forgot*. New York: Brassey's, 1994. A classic work on the French defeat that altered American policy toward Southeast Asia and led to U.S. involvement in Vietnam.

John T. Smith, *The Linebacker Raids: The Bombing of North Vietnam, 1972*. London: Arms and Armour, 1998. A concise account of the last U.S. major aerial campaign of the Vietnam War.

Ronald H. Spector, *After Tet: The Bloodiest Year in Vietnam*. New York: Free Press, 1993. A brilliant narrative account of all aspects of the bloodiest year of the Vietnam War.

Mike Spick, *The Ace Factor*. New York: Avon, 1988. A cogent analysis of the elusive ability that sets an ace apart from his comrades-in-arms.

———, *The First Cav in Vietnam: Anatomy of a Division*. Novato, CA: Presidio, 1987. Recounts the development, testing, and battles of essentially the first helicopter air-assault division (Airmobile).

———, *Rangers at War: LRRPs in Vietnam*. New York: Ballantine, 1993. The story of the elite U.S. Army Rangers performing tough, danger-filled long-range reconnaissance patrols in Vietnam.

Shelby L. Stanton, *The Rise and Fall of an American Army: U.S. Ground Forces in Vietnam, 1965–1973*. Novato, CA: Presidio, 1985. The first total battlefield history of ground forces, year by year, front by front.

———, *Green Berets at War: U.S. Army Special Forces in Southeast Asia, 1956–1975*. New York: Ballantine, 1999. The combat history of the legendary U.S. Army Special Forces.

———, *Historical Atlas of the Vietnam War*. Boston: Houghton Mifflin, 1995. An incisive examination of the Vietnam War that autopsies its myths and misconceptions and lays bare the skeleton in America's closet.

Harry G. Summers Jr., *On Strategy: A Critical Analysis of the Vietnam War.* Novato, CA: Presidio Press, 1982. Required reading for anyone interested in U.S. military strategy not only in Vietnam but also around the globe.

———, *Vietnam War Almanac.* New York: Facts On File, 1985. A well-researched and well-written chronicle and encyclopedia of the Vietnam War by a former colonel of infantry in Vietnam.

John Trotti, *Phantom over Vietnam: Fighter Pilot, USMC.* Novato, CA: Presidio, 1996. A veteran of six hundred combat missions over Vietnam tells it like it was in a thundering jet fighter.

James R. Wilson, *Landing Zones: Combat Vets from America's Proud, Fighting South Remember Vietnam.* New York: Pocket, 1993. An oral history of the Vietnam War, compiled, arranged, and authored by a former staff officer in Vietnam.

Mark W. Woodruff, *Unheralded Victory: The Defeat of the Viet Cong and the North Vietnamese Army, 1961–1973.* Arlington, VA: Vandamere Press, 1999. The true—but rarely acknowledged—history of the defeat of the Viet Cong and NVA forces by U.S. forces and their allies during the Vietnam War.

Marilyn B. Young, *The Vietnam Wars, 1945–1990.* New York: HarperCollins, 1991. An engaging account of the events of the war, with a keen analysis of America's decision to make war in Southeast Asia.

★ Index ★

★ Picture Credits ★

Cover photo: AP/Wide World Photos

© Robin Adshead; The Military Picture Library/Corbis, 33

AP/Wide World Photos, 7, 22

Archive Photos, 9, 10, 12, 25, 26, 29

© Bettmann/Corbis, 15, 16, 18, 24, 31, 34, 41, 47, 48, 58, 59, 60, 63, 68, 72, 76, 78

© Corbis, 30 (right), 35, 38, 40, 43, 67

Courtesy United States Navy, 62

FPG International, 51, 53

© George Hall/Corbis, 52, 65

© Hulton-Deutsch Collection/Corbis, 74

National Archives, 30 (left), 37

© Tim Page/Corbis, 36, 70, 75

© Leif Skoogfors/Corbis, 13, 14, 54

© Nevada Wier/Corbis, 71